D0171533

# Contents

∞

# Acknowledgments

THIS BOOK HAS BEEN FIFTY-SIX YEARS IN THE MAKING. I'd like to thank those upon whose broad shoulders I've stood in order to make my dreams a reality. I'd like to acknowledge:

Don Miguel Ruiz for his wisdom, friendship, and unconditional love. Miguel, in all the years we've been together, I can't recall a single unkind word shared between us. I'd also like to thank the Toltec teachers, for all the learning and laughing we've shared as we've journeyed together.

My mom—you've supported me unconditionally from the moment of my breechy entrance into this world. Thanks for believing in me when others didn't.

Gramps, you were the light of my life and still live in me.

Marshall Thurber for being my first teacher, encouraging me to teach and to become a systems thinker. Bucky Fuller for your humanity and easily shared genius. W. Edwards Deming for giving me my foundation in systems. Ernest Holmes for your introduction to the workings of the mind. *A Course in Miracles*, just for being. Muktananda and Gurumayi for my introduction to Eastern teachings. Alvaro and Gabriella Lopez Watermann for DreamWork and the ability to understand the powerful messages that snuggle in every sleeping dream. My friend and mentor, Carm Santoro, for sharing with me your wise insights in to the wonderful world of business.

My East Coast "Dream Team" who grabbed this work and this book and wouldn't let go until it was a reality, including: Joanne Dunleavy, my coaching guru; Kevin Murray, CEO and teacher extraordinaire; Ed Lay Jr., my visionary publisher at the Emeritus Group; Caroline Young, Cyndie Koopsen, and Gail

Fink at ALLEGRA Learning Solutions, who helped me piece hundreds of pages into a coherent manuscript; Lois Stanfield, for her elegant interior design; Christinea Johnson, who jumped in with all her heart with her energized cover art and general book-making expertise; and James Clark for your gift of public relations based upon The New Agreements.

My family, who have been the rock upon which I've stood: My handsome sons, Steve and Mike, for loving me in spite of my "far-out" dad ideas. My beautiful daughter, Quinn, for loving me and allowing me to love her back. And lovely Linda, my wife of thirty-one years. What an inspiration that we could walk this path together.

And finally, I want to acknowledge *you*, the new leaders and warriors who will make the release of the creative human spirit in the workplace a reality. I'm honored to have you by my side.

*David Dibble*

# Foreword

TEN YEARS AGO, DAVID WAS WITH ME ON ONE OF MY
power journeys to the Toltec city of Teotihuacan. At
that time, he was struggling, trying to keep his business alive after having lost all interest in what he was
doing. His lack of interest in his business caused
extreme tension in his life.

One night we had a very interesting conversation.
First, I showed him the power of the will, and I let
him know that this power could be used in any direction of his life to accomplish anything he ever
dreamed of accomplishing. I let him know that he
was already a great master, and that he could have
anything he wanted if he just used his will to reach

his heart's desires. At the same time he had to be completely detached from whatever it was that he wanted.

Many years later, David discovered for himself that just by controlling his will, he was able to get everything he wanted, but at the same time, he learned to be detached from all the things he did not need. He began sharing this gift with whoever was ready to hear his message, and the focus of his message was the workplace, because the workplace is his passion. After years of teaching people his valuable business skills, his experience brought about the creation of a small, simple, but very powerful book about transformation of the workplace.

In this book, David describes the workplace as a wonderful dream that for many has become a nightmare. This dream is alive and constantly changing, depending upon the needs of its leaders. David saw how the nightmare could be changed back into a wonderful dream. Something that used to be complicated for him became very simple, and the key to this simplicity is detachment from the outcome. At the same time, David uses his strong will to be a model of what he teaches.

*The New Agreements in the Workplace* will touch your heart. If you are ready for the next step in your workplace, this book holds the energy to start your journey. Read the words in this book with an open heart, and see if you begin to feel the release of your creative human spirit. The journey to mastery in the workplace may begin with the wisdom in these pages, and I highly recommend that you put into action the principles in this book to begin your own transformation at work and at home.

*Miguel Angel Ruiz*

# INTRODUCTION

*"Depression occurs when you catch a sudden insight into the emptiness
of your life. A man thinks he is happy with all his business and social
activities. But he catches a glimpse that it is all an act, which depresses him.
It is like dreaming about a palace and waking up in a mud hut."*
—VERNON HOWARD

IN 1980, I WAS LIVING THE AMERICAN DREAM. I OWNED
a successful company and was surrounded by wealth.
I had a big house, a jet black turbo-charged 928
Porsche, a beautiful wife and two sons, real estate,
stocks, and many friends. Life was one big party,
filled with an exciting nightlife and more than a little
self-indulgence. I had everything a man could want,

but somehow I felt empty and lost. Even my attempts to numb myself with drugs and alcohol failed to ease my longing. I was close to misery.

Then in February I had an intense spiritual awakening, and life as I knew it blinked out of existence. I was sitting on my living room couch and my grandfather (who had passed away) appeared to me, just as clearly as could be, standing right in front of me. I had never been so scared in my life. I thought I had gone insane, and I burst into tears. Gramps simply stood there and said, "David, what are you doing?" Simple question, no judgment. As I started telling him about my life, he disappeared. I thought, *Oh my God, I've got to get off the sauce, I've got to do something different. Maybe I'm going crazy.*

I thought the episode was over, but then my grandfather appeared again. He was wearing the same threadbare maroon sweater he had always worn, and he was standing right in front of me. He had a big smile on his face and he said, "David, you're not alone." For the first time in my life, I realized the truth of that statement. I was not alone. I was loved.

In the ten short minutes that followed, my destiny was revealed with crystal clarity, and there was no turning back. Suddenly I knew, beyond the shadow of a doubt, that I was meant to teach. My body collapsed into a heap, and heavy tears of shame and grief ran hot against my cheeks as I examined my life. Then came new tears of happiness and gratitude for my awakening.

With eyes of shimmering grace, I went to my wife, Linda, and took her into my arms. Asking for a second chance, I recommitted myself to my family. Even though my sons were only toddlers, I went to them and promised to be a better dad. I quit everything that day—the alcohol, the drugs. I shed my old life like a useless skin and began to shape a new reality—a reality that expressed my full humanity, spirit, and joy.

So began my quest for enlightenment. It was time to know my inner truth.

As a seeker of truth for over two decades, I have walked a number of passionate paths. Ultimately, I was led to the one that has since become my own: the Toltec path.

There are many paths to enlightenment, and each person can and should choose the one that suits him or her best. I am not here to say that one path is better or more worthwhile than another; the Toltec path is simply the one that works best for me personally, and upon which this book is based.

Until recently, few people knew about the Toltec outside of a few master teachers and the small groups of apprentices who studied with them. One such teacher is DON Miguel Ruiz, author of the best-selling books *The Four Agreements* and *The Mastery of Love*, which contain many of the basic tenets of the Toltec teachings. In the pages that follow, you'll find a brief overview of the Toltec teachings, just enough to lay the foundation for the real work of this book. If you want to learn more about the Toltec, I highly recommend both of DON Miguel's excellent books.

I've been graced with some amazing mentors and guides, but DON Miguel stands above the rest. For eight years, he guided me on the Toltec path to personal freedom. Then in 1998, DON Miguel and I agreed that it was my turn to guide others to their own truth.

As I set myself to my new mission, I came to an important realization. Finding our own personal path and making our own transformation is a crucial first step, but it is only the beginning. In order to live in a world of peace and productivity, we need to effect a *global* transformation as well. We need to change our world from a place of fear to a place of love.

The world we live in is changing so rapidly that we must constantly evolve just to keep up. Explosions in technology have turned yesterday's dreams into today's reality. Yet the very things that were supposed to bring us more freedom, comfort, and leisure time have resulted in a world where people spend more time and energy "on the job" than ever before. As a result, we want and need our workplaces to be environments in which we can learn, grow, and contribute. Even more important, we need a new kind of leader to guide us through these tumultuous changes.

As a former CEO, management consultant, and systems thinker, I believe the solutions to our problems lie in the way we conduct business and run organizations. We cannot make the important shift from fear to love without a transformation in the workplace. Only then will we see our world become a place of true humanity, spirit, and joy. We can make such a miracle happen in our own lifetimes. We must!

The workplace may have to take the lead in this coming global transformation. The teachings of the Toltec, along with some simple changes in the way we do business, can act as a practical road map for transforming the workplace and releasing the human spirit as our most productive and creative resource.

*The New Agreements in the Workplace* offers a process that integrates personal growth and personal freedom with a method of management based upon systems thinking and reexamining obsolete agreements and habits that are taken for granted in the workplace. In this book, you'll be introduced to systems theory, and you'll learn the five simple agreements that produce both joyful employees and successful organizations. You'll also discover a revolutionary idea that focuses on something seldom seen but desperately needed in the modern business world: love.

This approach is about going to a whole new level of being where the old systems/agreements, the people, and the environment are based on a new reality, a new possibility for the workplace. No matter what position you hold in your workplace or organization, the information you're about to learn will help prepare you to take your place as one of the new leaders. Whether you're an educator, health-care professional, researcher, artisan, business leader, administrator, manager, or employee in any type of organization, you will be able to apply the teachings of this book to your life and your workplace, to produce the kind of results you've only dared to imagine.

# 1

# Today's Changing Workplace

*"The idea that to make a man work you've got to hold gold in front of his eyes is a growth, not an axiom. We've done that for so long that we've forgotten there's any other way."*
—F. Scott Fitzgerald

CONVENTIONAL BUSINESS MODELS PORTRAY THE workplace as nothing more than an assortment of divisions, units, departments, or functions—boxes on an organizational chart. The people working within the boxes are seen as separate parts of the business machine, with little connection to the whole.

According to the traditional, top-down model of business, here's how an organization should work: Leaders lead and everyone else follows. The boss sets things up. The employees do what they're told. The boss is always right and the boss is always in charge.

We know that the minds of the organization's leaders tend to shape the mind or culture of the business. If the leaders' minds are run by beliefs, or what I call *agreements*, based on fear and control, the organization's mind will be made up of many of those same fear-based agreements. Unfortunately, fear-based agreements are rarely challenged. Instead, they are often taken for granted as "just the way work is done."

Without even realizing it, you've probably come across some of these fear-based agreements yourself. See if you can fill in the blanks in the examples that follow. (You probably won't need them, but you'll find the answers at the end.)

1. Give 'em an inch and they'll take a _____.

2. To get along, _____ along.

3. Cover your _____.

4. It's the boss's way or the _____.

5. Do what I say, not what I _____.

6. Leave your problems at the _____.

7. Follow the _____.

8. If you can't do the job, there's _____ out there who can.

9. We're not paying you to _____.

10. Don't make _____.

11. If his lips are moving, he must be _____.

12. They're lazy. They're just picking up a _____.

13. There's plenty more where they came _____.

14. In business, the only thing that matters is the _____.

*(Answers: 1 Mile; 2 Go; 3 Ass; 4 Highway; 5 Do; 6 Door; 7 Rules; 8 Someone; 9 Think; 10 Waves; 11 Lying; 12 Paycheck; 13 From; 14 Bottom line.)*

These and other fear-based beliefs exist both in the minds of people in the workplace and in its systems and policies. Workers at many levels feel powerless and controlled. They trudge on day after day, picking up their paychecks and paying their bills. This is called work. While not all workplaces are like this, to varying degrees, many are. Even the "good" places to work often fall far short of what's possible when the creative human spirit is allowed to be released in the workplace.

As a result, many people—from CEOs and top executives to businesspeople and minimum-wage workers—feel that America is "going down the tubes" from a *values* standpoint. Most also feel that their personal future prospects are becoming dimmer because they have to work harder just to maintain their current standard of living. The feeling for most of us is that our children are going to have a tougher time making it than we did. This worries us.

As a nation, America grows more and more fearful by the day. Unless we change direction, our problems will only become more acute. Like attracts like. Fear attracts that which we fear. Today's rapidly evolving world demands a new approach. It's time to choose a new, more benevolent energy, an energy that can *always* be trusted to take us to the right place. That energy is love.

Increasingly, organizations and businesses are discovering that the workplace must be more than just an environment for producing, marketing, and selling a product or service.

Successful organizations are those in which employees feel nurtured and supported, where personal growth is part of the business plan, and where each individual believes he or she makes a meaningful contribution. In successful organizations, systems are set up to help people be the best they can possibly be and to experience their full humanity and creative potential. That attitude is transmitted to the customers or clients, who demonstrate by their patronage that they would rather do business in a positive environment than in a negative or neutral one.

## THE SECRET INGREDIENT

BILL GALT IS ONE OF THE MOST BRILLIANT AND LOVING men I've ever had the pleasure to call my friend. As the founder of The Good Earth restaurants, he dreamed of providing healthy, great-tasting, impeccably served meals in a loving environment. Through his vision, he created an atmosphere where cooks put love into everything they prepared and the wait staff put love into everything they served. Customers were treated to an environment where love was served up as the special of the day, every day.

People who ate at The Good Earth restaurants came away talking about how good it felt to eat there, how tasty the food was, and how wonderfully they were treated by the employees and staff. High-profile companies held strategic and creative meetings at the restaurant because "ideas just seemed to flow" there. Celebrities showed up to be in the energy and stayed long after the kitchen closed, telling stories or reciting poetry.

Employees of The Good Earth thought of it as "home" and "family," and they absolutely loved their jobs. People lined up to apply for positions, but there was virtually no turnover. Yes, there was something unique about The Good Earth.

When asked to explain what made his restaurants so special, Bill Galt's answer came easily: It was love. And Bill will tell you today, "We put our love into everything we did. That's what made all the difference."

Eventually, Bill sold his chain of restaurants to a Fortune 500 company and joined the board of directors. The new owners knew they had a good thing going, and they didn't alter much. However, as with any acquisition, they felt compelled to put in some controls.

Things began to change. For no apparent reason, revenues began to drop and costs began to rise. Customers noted that something was "different" or "missing" in The Good Earth. Employee turnover increased. For the first time in the company's history, franchisees began filing lawsuits.

The board members asked Bill what he thought the problem might be. Their jaws dropped when he told them the esoteric yet profound truth: The company had lost the energy of love as its guiding principle. The environment had been compromised in the name of control. Everyone could feel it, even if they couldn't articulate it.

The solution to the problem? Love!

The new owners did their best to turn things around. They hired Bill to take a team of people back into the restaurants and help restore the energy. This strategy worked in certain locations for a while, but in the end, control won the day and The Good Earth became a good dining experience, not the "out of this world" experience it once had been. I still enjoy eating at The Good Earth. The food is wholesome and the service is usually good. But I miss the poetry.

## WHY WE KEEP DOING WHAT DOESN'T WORK

I TELL THE STORY OF THE GOOD EARTH RESTAURANTS to illustrate what happens when business domestication wins the day. What do I mean by domestication?

From our earliest infancy, our parents tell us how things are and must be. Since we're too small to resist, we have no choice in the matter. Later, our teachers, our peers, and society as a whole contribute to the message. We think that we think for ourselves, but we don't. This process by which the beliefs of our predecessors tend to become our own is called *domestication.*

Just as schools and society support the domestication of individuals, businesses support the domestication of people in the workplace. Leaders and managers learn what it takes to get ahead or simply survive in their organizations, then they pass that knowledge down through successive generations of leaders and managers as the unquestioned "way that it is."

Business policies such as fear-based command-and-control structures, manipulation of generally accepted accounting practices, a focus on shareholder value, and restructuring at the first sign of a downturn are examples of fear-based practices that keep organizations domesticated, unable to think outside their old belief systems. At its worst, domestication leaves a legacy of fear and conformity that creates a life experience far short of the joy and happiness that are truly possible.

With our world seemingly becoming more fearful every day, it's time to awaken from our domesticated slumber and become aware of a whole new possibility: a world based on love rather than on fear. I'm talking about nothing less than transforming our current fear-based workplace model into one based on love, one that is aligned with the Universal Creative Energy that exists in each and every human being.

## VISION: A DREAM, OUR DREAM

IN *THE WIZARD OF OZ*, WHEN DOROTHY CONFIDED TO Toto, "I don't think we're in Kansas anymore," she may have been expressing the same dilemma that America faces. We are entering an unfamiliar new reality and, like Dorothy, we first need to realize that the old rules no longer apply. We need a new vision, a vision of the heart.

Visions are vivid dreams that focus and inspire people and organizations to reach for the stars. Visions are real; they are alive. We can feel visions in our hearts and throughout our bodies. When we share our vision, others are moved by our passion and sincerity.

Everything is created twice: first in the mind, then in the physical domain. What if we could clearly envision our organizations as centers of enterprise and learning where people became healthy physically, emotionally, and spiritually? What if our dreams included powerful energy fields of love that would radiate from our people to each other, including our customers, clients, suppliers, stockholders, families, and community? What if we could become a living model for the full and human potential of work? What if we could dare to dream the impossible dream?

This is a call to a rousing of the heart, a heart awakening to a great possibility. The only requirement is that you be who you are and who you have always been—a loving human being—and that you share yourself with others who are ready for the change. Have courage. Be real. Trust your feelings. Tune out the talk-show chatter in your head and hear the glorious symphony that plays perfectly in every heart. Make your workplace an extension of love, the universal and unconditional love that connects all humanity to each other and to the stars. Build it in this way and your dream will come to you—and you and your people will prosper and be happy.

Albert Einstein envisioned a strategy that puts people before technology and intellect. Nothing short of a people-first philosophy will drive successful enterprises in the near future.

In the pages that follow, you will learn about five simple agreements. Keeping these agreements with yourself in your personal and professional life will ensure your place as one of the new leaders in today's changing workplace. If you're ready to begin, then turn the page and let's discover the New Agreements in the Workplace:

1. Find Your Path

2. Love, Grow, and Serve Your People

3. Mind Your Mind in the Moment

4. Shift Your Systems

5. Practice a Little Every Day

∞

# 2

## FIRST NEW AGREEMENT

# Find Your Path

*"Whatever you can do or dream you can, begin it!*
*Boldness has genius, power and magic in it."*
—GOETHE

As individuals in the workplace and in the world, each of us must find our own path to personal freedom and personal transformation. This step is so important that I've made it number one in *The New*

*Agreements in the Workplace.* Before you can hope to effect change that involves other people, your workplace, or your systems, you must first and foremost find your own personal path and begin to experience the personal renaissance of a transformed life.

Organizations, too, will benefit greatly in finding a collective path. Organizations must look for a path that is inclusive. An organization might be pulled to becoming a New Agreements company or a Four Agreements company or a Golden Rule company or might decide, "Our path is to release the creative human spirit in all we do." Paths like these are similar to an organizational vision or mission, but unlike most corporate visions and mission statements, which tend to be little more than nice-sounding words, a true path has the potential to provide real meaning, guidance, and values for people.

It's relatively easy to collectively get behind the New Agreements or the Four Agreements. We'd probably all agree that it's right to treat people as we would like to be treated. Most of us would likely support the "release of the creative human spirit in all we do." These are paths that support both the organizational and individual journey and thus have the power to align people in a common cause.

## Finding A True Path

There are many paths to freedom, and all true paths lead from fear to love, from separation to integration. Anything that creates more separation is not a true path. Because all true paths are very much alike at their essence, you may ultimately decide to incorporate into your own personal path the teachings of Jesus, Buddha, Muhammad, Moses, Krishna, and the great saints who have graced our world.

Once you've found your path, be careful not to impose it on anyone else. You may choose the Toltec path and think it's great, but if that's your choice, it would be wrong to try to impose this choice on others. You must remember that people will be naturally pulled to their path when the time is right.

Anytime you push, you're going in the wrong direction.

Some paths may present the opportunity of working with a true teacher. If you are fortunate enough to find a true teacher, this is a blessing of the highest order. A true teacher will have the ability to greatly accelerate your journey on your chosen path to personal freedom. But remember, as you grow, don't become dependent on any one person, philosophy, or methodology. We don't need more gurus. We must become our own gurus.

Although this is not absolutely necessary to begin your journey, seek a transformational experience that "lights your light," one that expands your consciousness in a profound and meaningful way. Look for an experience that shows you a whole new reality, a deeper sense of your true essence. This powerful experience might be a journey to a sacred place of spiritual power like the ancient Toltec city of Teotihuacan, a transformational retreat or workshop, or something as simple as spending time with a true teacher. As you light your inner light, your workplace becomes brighter and brighter from your radiance.

The path to freedom need not be a solemn one. Although deeply meaningful, your path should also be light, fun, and ultimately, human. If you're not laughing a lot, you've probably made things a little too serious. Lighten up (no pun intended)! Laugh. Enjoy. Love with every cell of your body.

With a little practice and grace, you may well discover *your higher purpose for work* along the way. Maybe you're going to transform the workplace from fear to love in your lifetime. Or maybe your higher purpose might be as simple and powerful as making a real difference in the lives of the children you teach. Regardless, a higher purpose for work will pop you out of bed in the morning knowing that your work is meaningful and valuable in the world and in your heart. This sure beats dragging yourself out of bed to pick up a check, waiting longingly for the weekend, or justifying poor performance to your board of directors.

A true path will provide practices, tools, and support on the journey to freedom and love. One such
path is the Toltec path. It is inclusive, simple, and
powerful, and because it is the one that I personally
follow, I've included a brief description of it in this
chapter. It is a proven path, but it is certainly not the
only way. The right path to freedom is the one that is
right for you. If you don't resonate with the Toltec
philosophies, keep looking until you find the path
that *feels* right for you.

## THE TOLTEC TEACHINGS

THE ANCIENT TOLTEC WERE NOT A TRIBE, BUT MORE
a band or community of like-minded individuals.
They were teachers, artisans, scientists, and thought
leaders who dominated central and southern Mexico
prior to the Aztecs, around the tenth to the thir-
teenth centuries. They had one thing in common: to
seek and preserve the spiritual knowledge passed
down from the ancient masters. This knowledge was

a universal knowledge and a path to personal freedom for those who practiced it.

According to Toltec philosophy, the sun's light is the source of information that tells our planet what to do. For example, in deference to Western science, the Toltec believe that the intelligence for the process of photosynthesis does not exist in the plant, it exists in the light that comes to the plant. The Toltec believe that our sun is the sixth in a series of suns since the beginning of time. Each sun produced a different quality of light; some have allowed fear to rule, while others have yielded heaven on earth. The most recent, the Fifth Sun, which ruled us for many thousands of years, was a fear-based one. However, with the coming of the love-based Sixth Sun in 1992, there is a change in the quality of the light, and fear is being transformed into love. This belief in the power of light is a central teaching of Toltec philosophy.

The Toltec built a city of pyramids forty miles northeast of Mexico City as a sacred place to live and practice their beliefs. They called this city Teotihuacan, which means "where one becomes God." The Toltec became known as "men and women of knowledge," but the knowledge they sought became a "Silent Knowledge" when it was driven underground during times of intolerance toward them. The Silent Knowledge survived by being passed down from master teachers called *naguals* to students who themselves became master teachers and continued to pass on this revered legacy.

When we talk about the Toltec philosophy, we are really talking about both a proven path to individual freedom and freedom of our humanity as an integrated whole. The Toltec philosophies involve three core Masteries. Out of these three Masteries, we can learn to live DON Miguel's Four Agreements. Integrating the three Masteries and the Four Agreements ultimately leads to one result: transforming fear into love.

## THE FOUR AGREEMENTS

AS I SAID EARLIER, *THE NEW AGREEMENTS IN THE Workplace* is based on the Toltec teachings in conjunction with some of my own experiences as a seeker of truth and a student of the workplace. Before we go any further, let's take a minute to review DON Miguel Ruiz's Four Agreements as his guide to personal freedom.

## Be Impeccable with Your Word

Speak with integrity. Say only what you mean. Avoid using the word to speak against yourself or to gossip about others. Use the power of your word in the direction of truth and love.

## Don't Take Anything Personally

Nothing others do is because of you. What others say and do is a projection of their own reality, their own dream. When you are immune to the opinions and actions of others, you won't be the victim of needless suffering.

## Don't Make Assumptions

Find the courage to ask questions and to express what you really want. Communicate with others as clearly as you can to avoid misunderstandings, sadness, and drama. With just this one agreement, you can completely transform your life.

## Always Do Your Best

Your best is going to change from moment to moment; it will be different when you are healthy as opposed to sick. Under any circumstance, simply do your best, and you will avoid self-judgment, self-abuse, and regret.

Now let's take a brief look at how the Four Agreements might apply in the workplace.

*1. Impeccability of the Word.* Impeccability of the word addresses the power of speaking with integrity. Possibly even more important, it means remembering to think before you speak and choosing words that come from love rather than fear. In some cases, being impeccable with your word means choosing not to speak if that is most appropriate to the situation. Can you see what this one agreement might do to reduce miscommunication, politics, and gossip in the workplace?

*2. Personal Affronts.* We must realize that what others say and think about us is not important. Their words, politics, and gossip have nothing to do with who we really are in the workplace. When we become unattached to what others say, think, and do, we need be concerned with only ourselves. This frees us to be more alive and energetic both in the workplace and at home.

*3. Assumptions.* Making assumptions is one of the fastest ways to create miscommunication and drama in our work lives. In most workplaces, we waste a great deal of time and energy dealing with politics, gossip, and solving problems that were created because we made assumptions that weren't true. We should take actions based upon good data whenever possible and avoid making assumptions, especially those that are fear-based.

*4. Best Work.* Most of us do the best we can under the circumstances. Our best will vary from time to time, but if we know we've done our best, we can be kind to ourselves regardless of the results we create. We must remember that we can be only as kind to others as we are to ourselves. In the new workplace, kindness to self and others will become a way of operating.

Can you picture everyone in your workplace being impeccable with their words? Not taking things personally? Not making assumptions? Doing their best all the time? Imagine what it would be like if everyone in *all* workplaces behaved that way.

Incorporating the Four Agreements into the workplace is a great idea, but they must become more than an idea or concept to bring value to the workplace. We must begin by practicing what we desire to become: We must become living role models and conduct our lives according to the Four Agreements. We must *be* the Four Agreements.

For those of you who are already using the Four Agreements as a guideline for improving your lives, you probably know how easy it is to forget to "live" the agreements. That's because the changes you're attempting to make are changes in your mind. Most of the time our minds run freely, spinning out thoughts, beliefs, and memories without our being a conscious part of the process. This is not such a good thing if our minds are full of fear-based thoughts, beliefs, and memories. Why? Because our minds often create a reality that is less than desirable, while we merely "go along for the ride."

How, then, do we begin to gain control of our minds so that we can have some control over what we experience in our lives? This is where the three Toltec Masteries come into play.

## THE TOLTEC MASTERIES

THE TOLTEC TEACHINGS INVOLVE THREE AREAS OF LIFE that must be mastered: Awareness, Transformation, and Intent. These Masteries are at the heart of the

Toltec teachings. When one becomes a master of Awareness, Transformation, and Intent, one masters life. A master of life creates the life he or she desires. A master creates heaven on earth. The Masteries are central to releasing the human spirit in the workplace, too.

## The Mastery of Awareness

The first Mastery involves waking up to the fact that you are not your mind. It means knowing that you are much more than what you think, believe, and remember. Without the Mastery of Awareness, virtually nothing is possible; your mind just runs on automatic pilot and you receive whatever comes along in life. But with heightened awareness, you can begin to work toward making your mind your ally. You can use your mind as a powerful, wonderful tool to enhance your life and the lives of others.

The purpose of your mind is to dream, to create your reality. Your mind is made up of your thoughts, beliefs, and memories. Your mind is that little voice in your head that constantly comments on everything you are and everything you do. When you're listening to your thoughts, you're listening to your mind. It's that little voice that may be saying, "What little voice?" or "I'd like to finish reading this, but I have to work."

In the beginning, there is much to listen to. But when you master this area of your life, you realize that you are not your mind. You understand that your mind is simply creating your reality and your dream. The Mastery of Awareness might also be called minding the mind, or the mastery of the moment.

Being aware of what your mind thinks, believes, and remembers gives you the chance to change your reality. *As on the inside, so on the outside.* In other words, everything happens inside out. To change your world, you must first change your mind. That's because your mind creates your reality or your "world."

If we're talking about changing the workplace, we're talking about changing the mind-set of that workplace, which is made up of the collective minds of all those in it. In either case, change starts with awareness.

Two types of awareness are critical in transforming the workplace. The first is an awareness of what your individual mind is up to. The second is an awareness of the *systems* that create fear in the workplace. Systems literacy (described in more detail later in this book) is crucial if you are going to achieve a Mastery of Awareness in your life and in the workplace.

The Mastery of Awareness is the cornerstone for every other Mastery. Nothing meaningful can be accomplished in the area of either personal transformation or transformation of the workplace without first obtaining some degree of Awareness. Without Awareness, the Four Agreements become nothing more than a nice concept instead of a practical guide to personal freedom.

Achieving the Mastery of Awareness requires three simple steps:

1. Catch yourself in the moment.
2. Observe what's going on inside and out.
3. Make a choice.

*Step 1: Catch Yourself in the Moment.* This first step is most easily explained by looking at an example. Let's say you frequently behave in an impatient manner and you'd like to do something about it. The first step is to start catching yourself at the moment you're feeling or behaving impatiently. Most people are pretty good at catching themselves after the fact, but looking back is an almost meaningless activity. All power exists in the moment when life is lived.

The key to changing is not to *try* to change, but first to become *aware* of what's happening *in the moment*. As a human being with little awareness, almost everything you do, you do automatically. You probably don't say to yourself, "I think I'll be really impatient because the person in front of me is writing a check in the cash-only line," or "I think I'll fail to delegate because I'm afraid of losing control." You just become impatient or fail to delegate when circumstances or something in the environment triggers that type of behavior in you.

If you do not become aware of your thoughts and the emotions or feelings that are a part of those thoughts, you have no chance of creating proactive change. On the other hand, if you can become *aware* of your thoughts and feelings in the moment, you gain a powerful advantage.

***Step 2: Observe What's Going on Inside and Out***. After becoming aware of how you are feeling, thinking, or acting, you can move to the next step of proactive change, which is to observe your thoughts and feelings. With awareness, you might say to yourself, "Oh, there are those feelings of frustration I get when people write checks in the cash-only line. This is my opportunity to watch both the situation and my reaction to it."

If you catch yourself behaving impatiently, feeling frustrated, or experiencing some other emotion that you'd like to change, simply stop for a moment and observe what you're doing, saying, thinking, or believing in that instant.

In the physical universe, the very act of observing something changes it. Science has discovered that two researchers cannot view the same event and "see" the same thing. That which is being observed is altered by the consciousness of those who are observing. The act of observing the mind begins to change that mind. This phenomenon offers significant opportunity to create proactive change in your life and in your workplace.

***Step 3: Make a Choice.*** As you become aware of your feelings, thoughts, and actions—and can observe them—you reach a most powerful place: the place of choice. In this place you can choose to be impatient or not. If you choose to be impatient, great; be really impatient. Roll your eyes, tap your foot, throw your hands up in exasperation. Whatever you do when you're really impatient, do more of it. Really get worked up. You might be pleasantly surprised to discover what happens when you exaggerate the thing you're trying to change. Many times you'll begin to see your "impatient routine," and that alone will take the edge off the experience.

You could also choose to be less impatient (we'll talk about how to do that in a moment when we discuss the Mastery of Transformation). Either way, you win.

The simple process of becoming aware and observing your thoughts and the accompanying feelings creates the option of choosing your actions. The more times you can observe the thoughts and emotions that normally cause your unwanted actions, and the more times you can choose your actions, the faster you will change.

Emotions, particularly those that are fear-based, are signals that call you to bring yourself into a state of heightened awareness. Whenever you become aware of a strong emotion, catch yourself in the moment, observe your behavior, and make a choice.

When your mind runs on automatic pilot, there's no movement toward transforming fear into love. You, not your mind, must make a choice. There are no right or wrong choices. The important thing is to decide how you're going to be or what you're going to do. If you're behaving impatiently, you can choose to continue that behavior or stop it. Always remember that choosing *to change or not to change* is still a step in the right direction. At least you're making a choice. As you will soon see, the choice itself is not as important as the *process* of making that choice.

## The Mastery of Transformation

After becoming aware of your thoughts, emotions, and behaviors, the next step is to choose different thoughts and beliefs, as opposed to the old fear-based ones that no longer work. Although greatly simplified here, this is the basis of the Mastery of Transformation.

When you become aware of energy-draining thoughts, beliefs, and memories, you can choose new ones based in love rather than fear. Fear or love, there's always a choice. Let's go back to our impatient example and look at a new set of thoughts that might serve you better.

You could choose to change your thoughts to something like the following: *That person writing the check probably didn't mean to make me wait. No big deal, anyway. The extra three minutes in line really won't affect me. Maybe the delay will prevent me from getting in an accident. Besides, this is a wonderful time to practice the Masteries of Awareness and Transformation. Actually, this whole experience is a gift.*

When you choose different, more loving thoughts, you're choosing to be less impatient. As you choose thoughts that are based more in love, you will find yourself proactively changing, transforming yourself into a new, more authentic person. Still, it will take commitment and effort on your part. Prison or freedom—it's your choice.

Unfortunately, your old beliefs are deeply rooted in something known as a *comfort zone.* Although the term suggests that a comfort zone is a place where you feel comfortable, that's not entirely accurate. It's possible to be miserable in your comfort zone. A more precise definition of a comfort zone is *a mental or phys-*

*ical place in which you know what to expect.* Regardless of whether you're comfortable, uncomfortable, miserable, or exhilarated, you feel like you know what to do, how to think, what to say, or how to feel.

Sometimes you're forced to reexamine the boundaries of your comfort zone. Imagine that you're about to do something you're not used to doing, something you don't know about. Perhaps your job requires you to make a speech, but you're not comfortable with public speaking. In such situations, the emotion of fear comes up immediately. If at all possible, you'll probably try to avoid doing the uncomfortable thing and retreat back to the center of your comfort zone.

What happens, though, if one day you go beyond your fears, into the unknown, and you make the speech? And then a few months later, you make another one? The unknown becomes the known. The fear may not disappear completely, but if you're willing to face your fears, eventually the new thing becomes known, familiar, and perhaps even comfortable. The end result is an expanded comfort zone.

The space between your old comfort zone and the new one represents *new freedom*. With an expanded comfort zone, you feel free to be more human and to experience life at a deeper level. As you continue to push the borders of your comfort zone, you begin to realize that you're experiencing your personal freedom. You can be yourself. This is an important part of the Mastery of Transformation. By changing your thoughts and overcoming your fears, you can escape from a fear-based environment and discover an expanded sense of personal freedom. When you know the truth about yourself, your comfort zone will stretch to the stars.

Our greatest possibilities lie in continually and consciously choosing to work through the fears that bind us. As Helen Keller said, "Life is a great adventure or nothing at all." Imagine if one of your life ambitions was to grow professionally, personally, and emotionally *all the time*; to constantly confront your fears and choose between comfort and freedom. Imagine what an adventure life would become if you choose freedom as often as you choose comfort.

Aware of the rewards and committed to attaining them, courageous people are those who push themselves toward the edge of their comfort zones, willing to go through the increasing amplitude of fear-based emotions. There are times, however, when we have no choice in the matter. Circumstances push us into the very areas of life that we have most dreaded, into those significant emotional events that take us to the edge and beyond our comfort zones, forcing us to face the prospect of transformation, whether we want to or not. In other words, the process of transformation is inevitable. But by mastering the areas of Awareness and Transformation, we can take charge of the process and make our own choices rather than letting our minds run on automatic.

## The Mastery of Intent

The third Mastery is the Mastery of Intent, which is really the mastery of energy. Quantum physics has shown that everything on Earth is made up of energy. What we used to think of as solid can be broken down into molecules, which are made up of atoms, which are made up of subatomic particles, which become nothing more than elements of energy. In other words, there are no solids; there is only energy.

When you master energy, you align yourself with the natural flow of the universe and the Higher Mind. The Mastery of Intent is really the mastery of love or the mastery of creation. When your mind is full of beliefs, thoughts, and memories that come from love, your mind aligns with the creative power that makes the stars shine. Intent is true magic.

You can send your Intent, your love, anywhere in the world at any time. You can send it through a thought or a prayer. You can send it through your eyes, your hands, a word, a touch. If you were to stop reading these words right now and send your Intent to someone you didn't even know—maybe a person who is gravely ill in a hospital in Australia or Zimbabwe—that person might very well heal more quickly. It is Intent that creates the healing.

Mastering the areas of Awareness, Transformation, and Intent is not a destination; it is a never-ending life process. It must be practiced, reinforced, and supported on a regular basis, optimally every day. Living the three Masteries will allow you to flow easily into the second New Agreement: Love, Grow, and Serve Your People.

# 3

## SECOND NEW AGREEMENT

# Love, Grow, and Serve Your People

*"All work is empty, save when there is love."*
—KAHLIL GIBRAN

THE WORKPLACE CAN BE THOUGHT OF AS A LIVING being. It is made up of people. If you took everything away from an organization but kept the people, the organization would still be "alive." The moment you remove the people from the organization, the organization ceases to exist.

When you love your people, you'll love your work. When you grow your people by helping them increase their capabilities and expand their skill sets, you'll grow the business or the organization. When you focus on loving and growing your people, they can focus on loving and serving your customers, your suppliers, and the world. Most important, love, growth, and service to others create an environment where you can release the creative power of the human spirit in your workplace. In this environment, "miracles" are not only possible, but also probable.

Of course, as you love, grow, and serve others, you will love, grow, and serve yourself in the process. It's said in some Eastern teachings that one can become a realized and enlightened being through the sole practice of service to others. This is a powerful agreement, especially for leaders and managers.

## MY JOURNEY

I WAS LUCKY ENOUGH TO LEARN THIS LESSON AT A very young age. As you may have already guessed, my grandfather was a special man. He was short, about five-feet-seven, even though he always claimed to be five-eight or five-nine. He was a wiry Scotsman and strong as an ox. He wasn't afraid of any man, and I had heard the stories about his prowess with a fist or an ax handle in the wild construction camps that he managed in his younger days. He had rightfully earned the respect of even the hardest of men. People were careful not to cross the man they respectfully referred to as Mr. Boyd, the man in charge of some of the most challenging construction projects ever designed in America.

I had heard the stories, but I never saw that side of my grandfather. Sure, he was strong and encouraged me to do more than I thought I could do. He would say, "You can do it, go ahead." But he was gentle, too. He could tell when I needed an arm over my shoulder, a kind word, a hearty laugh.

I was asthmatic as a kid, small and scrawny for my age, and not very athletic. Gramps, being a "water man," taught me to swim when I was five. A few years later we were swimming beyond the breakers when an acute asthma attack left me unable to breathe. I fought to stay afloat, struggling mightily for each constricted breath. "Gramps, I can't breathe!" I gasped. He shouted back, "Swim over to me and I'll help you in." Thrashing the water with growing panic, I inched my way toward him. Stretching to reach him, I felt my body sink into the choppy gloom. Fighting my way to the surface, I reached and sank again.

My throat was closing; every attempt at breath brought more water. I reached for him again, begging. No luck. He always seemed to be just out of my grasp. The battle for breath was lost, my energy exhausted. Just when I knew I could go no farther, I felt something strange brush against my foot, and then again. My God, it was sand! I was standing on the sand. Gramps had been moving toward the shore, staying just out of my reach until I made it in on my own.

Gramps took my arm, pulled me to his chest, and walked me the rest of the way to shallow water. He held my hand while I remained bent over in knee-deep water trying to catch my breath. Finally, he kneeled down and looked up at me. Wiping the tears from his eyes, he said, "I knew you could do it. Now you know you can do it, too. No matter what happens, no matter how hard it is, you can always make it if you don't give up."

Looking back, I think letting me struggle like that might have been one of the most difficult things my grandfather ever did for me. I think he was scared. He was very quiet the rest of the day and made it a point to put his arm around me more than usual.

Gramps was like that. He never gave up. He never stopped believing in himself or in me. We were partners. Together, we grew watermelons in the vacant lot next door. We chose just the right one, split it open, ate it, and thoroughly enjoyed the mess we made, the bigger the better. We laughed a lot. Gramps was genuinely interested in my view of the world. We would walk along the cliffs on narrow sandy trails high above the rocks and surf that posed more than a little threat to those less surefooted. We ate sour grass together and had contests to see who could stand chewing the biggest mouthful for the longest period of time. I think he let me win and pretended he couldn't take it.

We were like that. We were partners from the day of my birth. He was my leader and my teacher, and what he taught me was the power of unconditional love through commitment and contribution to others.

What does all this have to do with loving, growing, and serving your people? Everything, actually. Loving, growing, and serving others is an act of loving leadership. Leadership was the relationship my grandfather had with me. I would have followed him anywhere, done anything for him, and always with a smile on my face.

Like Gramps, the new leaders who take charge of our changing workplaces will lead from the heart, *pulling* their people with them as a part of their contribution. These new leaders will pull their followers to them because real caring is magnetic. No one will be pushed. Sure, the new leaders will be tough in their commitment to their people just like my grandfather was with me. But he was always there to catch me. He would never have let me fail.

The new leaders won't let their people fail, either. The new leaders will be models for their people. They will speak their truth and walk their talk, not because they are trying to impress anyone, but because that is who they are. They will *know* that there is no greater gift they can give themselves than to contribute to others from a place of personal integrity and unconditional love. They will constantly practice the second New Agreement in the Workplace: Love, Grow, and Serve Your People.

## LOVE YOUR PEOPLE

LOVE IS ATTRACTIVE. IT IS MAGNETIC. THE EMOTIONAL energy that emanates from love is one of the most powerful forces on earth. It literally opens up parts of ourselves that we may not have felt since we were little children, those joyful, playful, "everything's funny" parts that may have appeared lost or even dead.

The amount of work, learning, or healing (both physical and emotional) that can be accomplished in the presence of a love-based energy field is mind-boggling. Have you ever played on a team, participated in a charitable endeavor, or taken part in a spiritual gathering that made you feel connected, joyous, or even ecstatic? Where even people who were not a part of the activities knew that there was something special about your group? How would you characterize such an experience? Probably in a very positive way. In fact, I'll bet you remember that experience as one of the best of your life. When you felt that way, you were experiencing the feelings that come from *love* and *inclusiveness*.

People, including customers and suppliers, are drawn to leaders and organizations that operate in a loving way. In an energy field of love, the workplace becomes more of a heaven on earth, rather than the "hell" that many of us experience in fear-based work-places.

It's easy to tell a love-based organization from a fear-driven one. Try this experiment. The next time you have the opportunity to visit a company for the first time, arrive ten or fifteen minutes early so you can sit in the lobby and monitor its energy. Don't read a magazine or work. Just sit quietly. Listen to how the receptionist answers the phone. Does it sound like she enjoys her job? Does it sound like she really likes talking to people? Does she make them feel like they are important? Does she check back with the guests who are waiting to let them know she hasn't forgotten them?

How is the lobby laid out? Is it warm or cold? Is it comfortable for visitors? When employees pass through the lobby, are they energized, happy, and friendly? Or are they low-energy, going through the motions, cold, or distant? Most important, *how do you feel*? Do you feel a sense of well-being? Or do you feel subtly agitated or uncomfortable? The feelings you experience may be quite subtle, but they are always there. You can be sure that whatever you feel in the lobby is part of the energy field of the rest of the company.

The energy found inside the workplace is also carried away from that workplace. Whether the people in an organization travel around the corner or halfway around the world, they carry the emotional energy of their company with them. That emotional energy hits the emotional body of everyone they meet. It is felt at a subconscious level. If they carry the positive energy of a love-based workplace, they will be attractive. If they carry the emotions that come from a fear-based workplace, they will be unattractive.

Think about how this applies to an organization's salespeople. Their emotional energy can quickly translate into either greater or fewer sales for their company. You can easily see why it's so important to send out salespeople and representatives whose emo-

tional energy is positive. But how can you make sure
that happens?

It all begins with you, the leader. You love others
so they can love others, and so we all can someday
wake up to the fact that we're all loving ourselves.
That's how love works. In a strong emotional energy
field that comes from love, *anything is possible*. It is in
this type of environment where we may experience
the release of the creative human spirit.

## GROW YOUR PEOPLE

PEOPLE ARE THE ORGANIZATION. TO GROW YOUR
people means to grow the capabilities and skill sets
of the organization. Growing your people might take
the form of ongoing and extensive training, rotating
to new responsibilities and challenges, matching
roles to what makes a person's heart sing, or providing opportunities for self-improvement.

Hal Rosenbluth and Diane McFerrin Peters
wrote an interesting book called *The Customer Comes*

*Second.* Who do you think comes first? The people in your company.

Research clearly indicates that your customers will feel the same way about your company as your people do about their work. There's just a lag period. If you have unhappy people in your company, it's only a matter of time before your customers will be equally unhappy.

If top management is fearful, it will be difficult to create a working environment that feels safe. Managers who are fearful need to control others. Employee empowerment is impossible if management doesn't care about the people. Coaching, teaching, and growing people will be experienced by fearful managers as a potential loss of control or a waste of time and money.

Symptoms of fear in top management include risk-averse policies, nasty internal politics, poor interpersonal skills, a "numbers" consciousness, and doing the "easy thing" instead of the "right thing." This fear tends to trickle down through the organization and drives out anyone who is *not* afraid. Transformation in the workplace can begin only when the top management leaders understand the importance and benefits of loving, growing, and serving their people.

## SERVE YOUR PEOPLE

IF YOU LOOK AT THE GREAT TEACHERS OF THE PAST— people like Jesus, Muhammad, and Buddha—you'll see a common characteristic: They all served others. Like them, we must become servants to the people in our organizations if we want to release the human spirit in our workplaces.

Service to others is a wonderful practice for self-realization. As we serve our people, they are free to do the best jobs possible in serving each other and our customers. When we serve, we are served.

The area of service is particularly useful for leaders and managers. People are inclined to be drawn to and perform their best for leaders who serve them.

Service to others requires a certain level of spiritual maturity, but attaining this maturity is well worth the practice and effort.

In the book, *Critical Path*, author R. Buckminster Fuller explained that the world could be made into a better place if we cared about each other and if we shared the resources available on the planet. He demonstrated that if all people shared all resources, *everyone* could live at a standard we might call middle class. This would include adequate food, clean drinking water, good housing, medical care, and education—while improving the environment with a little good science and common sense. Even though his book contradicted what I "knew" about the world of business, much of *Critical Path* made sense to me intuitively.

In *The Fifth Discipline*, author Peter M. Senge further illustrated the challenge and promise of an inclusive society with the following statements by Albert Einstein:

> ... *[the human being] experiences himself, his thoughts and feelings as something separated from the rest—a kind of optical*

*delusion of our consciousness. This delusion is a kind of prison
for us, restricting us to our personal desires and to affection for a
few persons nearest to us. Our task must be to free ourselves from
this prison by widening our circle of compassion to embrace all
living creatures and the whole of nature in its beauty.* (p. 170)

What Einstein expressed so eloquently is the idea
that we human beings have tended to see ourselves as
individuals, separate from the rest of the human race.
Yet we know this illusion of separation is simply
incorrect. In essence, anything we do to others, we do
to ourselves. He makes a powerful case for following
the Golden Rule: Do unto others as you would have
them do unto you. So, what could possibly prevent us
from loving, growing, and serving our people?

## Fear—The Killer in the Kingdom

The human spirit is our unbridled life energy,
our aliveness, and the expression of our full and rich
humanity. Without the emotions that stem from love,
and the intelligence and information of light, renew-
al is not possible. Without love, there is much to fear.

Like the relentless, engulfing waters that can eventually cause a person to drown, fear causes our energy to slowly ebb away, withering our will to survive and eventually pulling our bodies into gloom. Fear attacks the very spirit of both people and organizations. Look for yourself, and you'll quickly discover that wherever you see problems that seem insurmountable, people are afraid.

Why don't we love our customers? Fear. Why do we have so much turnover? Fear. Why can't we work together? Fear. Why don't we change—*really* change—our organizations? Fear. Why is morale so low? Fear. Why are politics so prevalent in the workplace? Fear. Why are male-female relationships so difficult? Fear.

When we replace the fear in our organizations with the emotional energy of love, growth, and service to others, we will see dramatic improvements in productivity, morale, creativity, quality, teamwork, and of course, sales and profits. You may be thinking that solving most of your unmanageable problems by loving, growing, and serving your people is simplistic. You're right. Love *is* simple, yet it's powerful. It knows no limits and will illuminate the darkness of ignorance wherever it shines. Love doesn't conquer; it gently embraces fear and guides it to lasting safety.

## CRITICAL MASS IS CRITICAL

IN ANY ORGANIZATION, THE MOST RADICAL AND powerful energy shifts occur when all employees simultaneously experience the transformation of fear into love. Short of that, it appears that an entire culture of a company can be guaranteed to shift if a critical mass of executives and managers have experienced the transformation.

It appears that when the top 5 to 15 percent of a company, *including top management*, have ignited the energy in themselves and are committed to the new vision, the entire culture will soon follow suit. It's no longer a matter of *if* the necessary changes can be effected; it's a matter of *when*. Literally, as the thoughts and beliefs of top and upper management shift, the culture of the organization begins to transform. It is in this realm of top and upper management that the second New Agreement in the Workplace—Love, Grow, and Serve Your People—has the greatest power for organizational transformation.

To become the type of leader who naturally loves, grows, and serves others, you must venture one step further, to the source of all emotional energy: your mind. Once there, you must practice until you master the third New Agreement in the Workplace: Mind Your Mind in the Moment.

∽∞∾

# 4

## THIRD NEW AGREEMENT

# Mind Your Mind
# in the Moment

*"The mind is its own place, and in itself
Can make a heaven of Hell and a hell of Heaven."*
—JOHN MILTON

SCIENCE HAS BEEN "LOOKING" FOR THE HUMAN MIND
for thousands of years with no success. Many of these
efforts have represented the mind and brain as one

and the same. Researchers have attempted in vain to make a mind-brain connection, some even going so far as to intimate that the mind somehow functions like the brain. It doesn't.

The brain is a physical organ that connects the mind to the outside world and the body. You probably would not want to do this (unless you're a pathologist or a brain surgeon), but you can actually hold a brain in your hands. It is a tangible, physical part of the human body, made up of physical energy. The mind, on the other hand, is composed of a different kind of energy. You can't hold the mind, you can't x-ray it, scientists can't even find it. The mind is made up of *emotional energy*.

Like a transducer that takes power from one system and supplies it in understandable form to a second system, the brain transforms physical energy into emotional energy and vice versa. For example, if your hand gets too close to a burning flame, your body sends out an urgent message in the form of physical energy. The brain translates the message into emotional energy and the mind thinks, *My hand is burning!*

Health and well-being are functions of the mind. Life experiences and the drivers of behavior (emotions) are also functions of the mind.

This leads to another interesting riddle: Where does emotion reside? The Toltec say it resides in the mind as thoughts, beliefs, and memories. Although scientists have been unable to pinpoint the location of emotion, some say it resides in the brain, and some think it lives in the mind. However, since science has not been able to locate the mind, the search will go on and the exquisite futility will continue—endlessly. Western science will never actually prove the existence of the mind or emotions because neither exists in the physical reality that binds all science. They're made of emotional energy that vibrates at a frequency beyond physical reality. Attempts to find the mind or measure emotion end up measuring only electricity, a physical energy.

Although the physical proof of their existence remains elusive, we know we have a mind and we know we have emotions. Luckily, most of us don't need proof of the mind's existence or the fact that we have emotions because we feel them. We just know.

## THE MAKING OF THE MIND

HUMANS COME INTO THE WORLD AS NEARLY MINDLESS newborns. This may sound like a derogatory state-ment, but nothing could be further from the truth. The mind of a newborn is small and virtually without fear. It contains no psychological wounds or emo-tional scars. Having a small, naturally love-based mind makes a baby's experience of life far superior to that of most adults. Unlike adults, babies don't have anything to worry about. They live life in the moment, as life takes place. Only fear in the mind traps us in the past or makes us apprehensive about the future. Only the mind embraces strongly held beliefs and opinions that must be defended at all costs.

The human mind is the most mighty creative force in humanity's toolbox. Every thought, belief, memory, and human experience resides in the mind and contains an emotional component. The strength of this emotional component is what gives a positive or negative value to each and every experience that exists in the mind. This positive or negative emotional energy determines whether we attract "good" experiences or "bad" experiences to ourselves.

Scientists estimate that we have somewhere between 12,000 and 70,000 thoughts per day. Obviously, we are not even aware of the majority of these thoughts. Why are we aware of some thoughts and not others? It has to do with the emotional content of the thought or belief.

We become aware of our thoughts when their emotional content is high enough to bring them into our consciousness. Enough emotion and the thoughts become conscious. A little more emotion and the thoughts become important. A large amount of emotion and the thoughts become an all-important, driving force in our lives. Too much emotion and we can't think straight.

Memories and beliefs, like thoughts, are also weighed by their emotional content. Memories with high emotional content are more easily recalled. Beliefs with strong emotional components tend to be strongly held beliefs.

The mind determines how we experience life and *drives our behavior*. The mind tends to filter out anything unlike itself—anything that goes against our current belief systems. This is something that happens naturally. Things that are different from the mind often become invisible; we just don't see them.

To change our experiences, we must change our minds. Is changing the mind a simple task? Yes! Is it easy? Hardly! But it can be done. This is why the third New Agreement in the Workplace, Mind Your Mind in the Moment, is so important.

## MIND YOUR MIND IN THE MOMENT

HAVE YOU EVER HAD AN EXPERIENCE WHERE, IN retrospect, you realized you had let your mind impact a situation? If you're like most people, you've probably had many such experiences. However, there's nothing more powerful than being aware of your mind *in the moment* when your reality is created and your life is lived. If you choose to follow the Toltec path, you have some powerful, effective, proven tools at your disposal. Perhaps the most important of these is the Mastery of Awareness, which you learned about in chapter 2. As you may recall, it includes three simple steps: Catch yourself in the moment, observe what's going on inside and out, and make a choice.

To make the New Agreements in the Workplace or DON Miguel's Four Agreements a part of your work life, start by catching yourself in the moment. Become aware of when you're *not* following the practices. Utilize your awareness and notice when your mind is not acting impeccably with your thoughts and words, when your mind causes you to take things personally, when your mind makes assumptions, and when your mind causes you to do less than your best.

Notice when you're *not* on your path or *not* loving, growing, and serving your people.

In the beginning, there's much to become aware of because the process of domestication has produced many fear-based thoughts, beliefs, and memories. Left to itself, the mind will automatically pull these into consciousness whenever circumstances trigger a reaction. Left unattended, the mind creates all action-reaction experiences of life, both "good" and "bad."

A crucial warning signal that can help you become aware of what your mind is up to now, in this very moment, is the emotion that comes from fear. Without awareness, your mind will produce fear-based thoughts, beliefs, or memories, and you will simply react to that emotional energy. Without awareness, this simple action-reaction process leaves you with no choice in how you feel and behave. However, when you become aware that strong emotions are signaling you to pay attention to what your mind is doing, you have begun to practice the

Mastery of Awareness in your personal and professional life.

Developing an awareness of your emotions as
they occur, in the moment, can be a real challenge
when you first begin to practice this New Agreement.
You may forget time and again to be in the moment,
noticing only in retrospect that your emotions and,
thus, your mind were in control. That's okay. It's
part of the process of growth and transformation.
With practice, you'll get better and better at being
aware of emotions in the moment.

Once you have become aware of what your mind
is thinking, the next step is merely to observe the
mind. Do your best to keep your focus on what your
mind is thinking, believing, or remembering. The
very act of observing the fear in your mind begins the
transformative process.

Finally, minding your mind in the moment means
making choices about the thoughts, beliefs, and
memories that you allow into your mind. You can
choose to be happy or unhappy, bored or excited,

courageous or afraid. The very act of choosing, even if the choice is fear, begins to dissipate the fear-based emotional energy that causes you to be less than your fully human self. Of course, a choice of love will speed the process dramatically.

## DECISION MAKING: IT'S IN THE EMOTIONS

SOMETIMES YOU MAY FIND THAT YOU ARE NOT MOVING forward in your life and your current thinking isn't providing what you want, yet you can't seem to change your thinking. It's as if you're stuck in some sort of groove, held in place by an invisible glue. If that's true, then there must be a releasing agent of some kind to get you unstuck!

Not only is there a glue that keeps you stuck and a releasing agent that will loosen it, but it turns out that they are one and the same.

*Emotion* is the mysterious factor that drives every decision you make and gives value to every event you experience. You know whether life is good or bad because your emotions tell you how you feel. Fear-based emotions keep you stuck, while love-based emotions release you and allow you to change.

The amount of change you experience in life is normally in direct proportion to the emotional content of your experience. Without an understanding and awareness of the emotions involved in your life, change becomes difficult and, in some cases, impossible to manage. This is why minding the mind is paramount in the transformational process. It's the same for decision making.

Even tough, "unemotional" managers make every decision based on emotions. Roger, an upper-level accounting manager at a large corporation, is comfortable with numbers but uncomfortable with his feelings and general people issues. Because he considers himself a logical and unemotional person, Roger makes decisions based on numbers. He doesn't realize that, rather than avoiding his emotions, he is actually choosing the emotion of feeling comfortable. His desire for comfort directs him to do the things to which he has become accustomed. He stays within his comfort zone.

To avoid feeling uncomfortable (another emotion), Roger avoids situations where he would have to feel intense feelings or rely on intuition.

Can you see how Roger's decision to be unemotional, logical, or tough is actually an emotional decision? Is he minding his mind when he makes decisions this way? Does he have any choice with his mind running the show? I'm afraid not.

As a leader or manager, you'll fool yourself badly if you downplay the importance of emotions in making decisions. Key executives will join or leave your company, and customers will buy or not buy your products and services, for only one reason: *emotion*. They may back up their choices with logical arguments, and in many cases, may believe they arrived at their conclusions logically; however, their logic came into play only after their emotions pointed them toward what felt most comfortable and away from what they feared.

## THE NATURE OF CHANGE

THE TOOLS FOR ATTAINING HIGH LEVELS OF ORGANI-zational quality, enhancing productivity, and implementing systems-based change management are straightforward and well known. It's not that we don't know what to *do* from a structural standpoint. Why is it, then, that most of our efforts to create change are under-performing and, in many cases, failing outright?

Our organizations are full of bright, energetic, intelligent, and experienced leaders who stumble when it comes to proactively changing themselves and their businesses. They know they have to change and most have committed intellectually to change, but for some reason, they seem to have difficulty when it comes to actually making change happen. Why? Two reasons.

First, many changes are accompanied by fear-based emotions that some leaders don't want to experience. As a change becomes imminent, their feelings of discomfort and fear intensify. As individuals, some people would rather die than face these emotions. Public speaking, fear of death, confrontation, rejection, loss of control, fear of failure, and public humiliation are a few of the fears that might fall into this "kill me first" category.

Second, some people's belief systems or paradigms are based on past experience. Once created, beliefs tend to be naturally resistant to change.

Managers and leaders are human beings, too. Like everyone else, they have fears they never want to face. In the organizational world, these fears generally revolve around the prospect of being out of control, having to deal with people problems, looking stupid or foolish, or facing public humiliation. Since resistance to change and fear are intimately intertwined, executives, managers, and workers alike will go to extraordinary lengths to avoid changing and facing their fears. It is this avoidance that makes changing the organization so time-consuming and arduous.

Finally, when all efforts to resist the changing environment are exhausted, we are forced to face our fears. Surprisingly, it is at that point when something profound occurs. We find ourselves feeling more alive and we discover that life goes on—but not in the same way. The intense emotions we experienced were directly linked to the speed of change. The greater the emotion, the greater the rate of change.

The most rapid changes in organizations are often precipitated by an environment of crisis. Look at your own life and you'll probably see that this is true. Think back to a significant emotional event that rocked your world. Maybe it was the breakup of a relationship, a severe financial setback, the loss or near loss of a loved one, or a near-death experience. Did you change as a result of this event? If so, did you change quickly? Did this event affect your thinking, your beliefs, or your behavior? Were there new benefits associated with the event or changes created by the event? The answer to all of these questions is probably a resounding "yes".

Just like individuals outside the business, organizational managers and leaders tend to hold on to their old ways of doing things until a crisis in the environment forces them to do otherwise. Suddenly, changes that they vigorously resisted in the past now become more easily accepted. But even in crisis, even when faced with the death of the company, many times management will not do the things it most fears. Logically, they may know and understand the need for change. Nonetheless, they find themselves in a state of emotional paralysis, unable to move until there is no other choice.

Unfortunately for those leaders who vigorously resist transformation in their organizations, there will soon be little choice. Fear-based organizations will be unable to compete with those based in love. Fear is going the way of the dinosaurs, but with a little twist: The dinosaurs died, while fear will be transformed . . . to love.

## LOGIC HAS NO POWER

AS YOU LEARNED EARLIER IN THIS CHAPTER, EVERY decision a human being makes is driven by emotion.

However, under most current business models, there is little place for emotion in the workplace. Employees are asked to leave their emotions at the door and to think, behave, and speak logically. In the business world, people often put logic—not emotion—on a pedestal. But logic is little more than an unemotional-sounding way to justify or explain emotionally driven decisions. Despite the rules and regulations that govern the business world, logic is limp and impotent. *It has no power over emotion.*

Let's look at an example of why this is true. Imagine that an event occurs. It could be any event at all. What you choose to believe about the event (your reasons) determines how you feel about it (your emotions). Your reasons may or may not be correct; someone else who observed the same event might develop a completely different set of emotions and reasons about it. So your reasons could be completely false, but your *emotions are absolutely, undeniably real.* Because emotion is real and reasons are false, emotion always wins over logic in determining behavior.

In case you doubt the preceding statement, try the following experiment. Imagine that you've been given a small cup of water. Now imagine that you've just been asked to put the water in your mouth, swish it around, and spit it back in the cup. What are you thinking right now? Do you think this is just a little bit disgusting? But wait, let's take it a step further. Suppose you are asked to drink what's in the cup. Or worse, suppose you are asked to trade cups with someone else and drink from that person's cup!

Stop for a moment and examine your reactions.

- What do you think?
- How do you feel?
- What emotions did you experience?

Now let's see what happens when we apply logic to the situation. We know that saliva is a natural fluid that serves many useful purposes. It makes swallowing easier, it helps promote digestion, and it keeps our mouths and throats from feeling dry.

Applying this logical knowledge to our little experiment, are you now ready to drink that nice cup of water and saliva? Probably not. Why? Because of the *emotions* you associate with the idea of saliva or spit. Perhaps as a child you were taught that spitting was disgusting, insulting, or rude. Or maybe as an adult you learned about germs, so now you might worry about catching a disease. All this is a part of your domestication.

We could discuss the merits of saliva all day long and you would still not want to drink from that cup. But what if, when I mention saliva, you start thinking about kissing someone you love? If saliva makes you think of kissing, and if you associate positive emotions with that activity, you probably don't feel disgusted at the thought of ingesting a little bit of saliva!

Whatever your beliefs, they are connected to emotions that cannot be easily overridden by logic. If you want to make a change in the way you think or behave, you need to start by changing your emotions, not your logic.

## THE PARADOX OF
## ORGANIZATIONAL CHANGE

THE CRITICAL ROLE THAT EMOTION PLAYS IN BOTH our personal and professional lives is in direct opposition to the philosophy of traditional American business, which says to its employees, "Leave your problems (emotions) at the door!" Businesses are much easier to manage if emotions are removed from the equation. Most businesspeople can run a few computer models and determine the quickest return on investment. Any competent deal maker can merge two companies on paper and determine what their combined value would be. But if you examine the prospects of combining two cultures that are driven by different emotional energies, the results become much less predictable.

One of the biggest challenges in business is usually managing people and proactively making changes as the business environment dictates. If executives lose sleep at night, it's probably because they are frustrated with people issues. "It's always something," they lament. That "something" is emotions.

With American organizations generally doing all they can to control emotions in the workplace, is it any wonder that they have such a difficult time changing? Yet, emotions are both the lock that keeps us trapped in the old way of doing things and the key that will release our human spirit. To examine this dilemma, we must first find the source of emotional energy.

## Energy and Quantum Physics

In the not-too-distant future, the new leaders of business will operate from more of a quantum perspective—one that acknowledges and uses the energies and interconnections that exist among all people and organizations. Minding the mind in the moment means being aware of your emotional energy in the moment.

According to quantum physics, everything in the universe is interrelated and connected to everything else. In other words, you have an effect on all the other people in your world. Actually, each of us has an effect on everything in the universe. But back to home base for a moment.

As you learned earlier, quantum physics has demonstrated that there are no solids. In each case, the "solid object" is actually 99 percent space. There is nothing solid about anything; there are only patterns of energy. Buckminster Fuller referred to all things that appear to be solid as energetic "pattern integrities." The human body, the mind, our world, and even you are all just wonderful patterns of energy.

## The Emotional Body

We are all, at certain times, aware of our physical bodies. The physical body is that physical energy we see when we look in the mirror. But we also experience other "bodies" made up of nonphysical energy. One of these bodies is the emotional body.

Think of your emotional body as a field of emotions that wraps invisibly around and through your physical body. It cannot be seen; it can only be felt. For practical purposes, you might equate it with your mind.

Your emotional body, like the emotional body of every other person, contains emotional energy that comes from both fear and love, and that energy is constantly being exchanged between persons. Since everything is connected to everything else, you are also connected to all others in this world *emotionally*.

Your emotional body constantly exchanges emotional energy with other emotional bodies and with the emotional body of the planet, which contains the combined emotions of all humans on Earth. How you are affected by this emotional energy depends on the type of emotional energy that you attract or emit. If your emotional body consists primarily of emotions that come from love, you will attract an abundance of empowering experiences. However, if your emotional body is full of fear, you will attract experiences that you define as negative.

## The Emotional Energy of an Organization

In an integrated, love-allowing, centered organization, connections are vast, fluid, and intimate. The energy that creates and holds the connections together is emotional energy, the energy of love in the form of relationships. This connective energy can only be felt; it may be articulated by the rational mind, but the rational description is not the same as the experience of connectedness.

You learned earlier that the emotional energy of an organization creates a field of energy that can be felt and experienced. When customers walk into the lobby of a business for the first time, they get a "feel" for the business. How they will experience a particular field of energy depends on the source of the energy. Does the company radiate love or does it radiate fear? If the emotional energy comes from love, it will feel good to be there, both for the people working in the organization and the customers they serve.

Consider what Margaret Wheatley observed in *Leadership and the New Science:*

*Recently, while doing work on customer service for a retail
chain, I asked employees to visit several stores. After spending
time in many stores, we all compared notes. To a person, we
agreed that we could "feel" good customer service just by
walking into the store. We tried to get more specific by looking
at visual cues, merchandise layouts, facial expressions—but
none of that could explain the sure sense we had when we walked
into the store that we would be treated well. Something else was
going on. Something else was in the air, we could feel it, we just
couldn't describe why we felt it.* (pp. 52–53)

Wheatley described the feeling of an emotional
energy field that comes from love. Energy fields like
this, good or bad, are created in every organization.
The big question for leaders is, does your organization create fields of energy that come from love or
from fear?

## LIKE ATTRACTS LIKE

YOU HAVE PROBABLY HEARD SOMETHING LIKE THE
old saying "What you give out is what you get back."
This principle of "like attracts like" is considered a
universal truth in many teachings. In the case of emo-

tions and the emotional body, like will attract like, fear will attract more fear, and love will attract more love. This principle is critical to understanding what the future holds for you individually, in your place of work, and even for the nation or the world community. It also gives new meaning to the need to mind your mind—at least, if you want to have a meaningful and prosperous future.

Until now, most people have had the tendency to view the future as one large event that will affect everyone. Nothing could be further from the truth. Each individual and every company has the ability to attract a definitive future to himself, herself, or itself. Your experience of the future will be predicated on the emotional content of that future. In other words, organizations and the future of organizations will be ruled by the emotional energy they emit. Fear-based futures, in which levels of profitability and growth tend to be low or nonexistent, will be experienced as unsatisfactory. Supportive futures, which produce companies that set new standards for prosperity, will create a general sense of well-being in those involved.

The emotional energy that you and your businesses send into the world will attract like energy to you. If your organization is primarily fear-based, fear-based energy and events will be pulled to your company. You can expect a higher level of drama in fear-based organizations. At the opposite end of the spectrum, companies that make the shift to love-based emotional energy will pull pleasant and more profitable futures to themselves.

The choice is yours, and it all begins with minding your mind in the moment. To make a real difference in the workplace, though, you must next learn to differentiate between two integrated and equally important aspects of the workplace: the people and the systems. Problems in the workplace are rarely just people problems; they're usually systems problems that contribute to people problems.

In the following chapter, you'll learn to distinguish the two and solve many of your organization's problems by utilizing the fourth New Agreement in the Workplace: Shift Your Systems. When that happens, you'll be positioned to create real transformation in the workplace that will allow spirits to soar.

∞

# 5

## FOURTH NEW AGREEMENT

# Shift Your Systems

*"Men have become the tools of their tools."*
—HENRY DAVID THOREAU

ALL ORGANIZATIONS HAVE STRUCTURAL COMPONENTS
that we call systems. Systems, for the most part,
direct how we do things. Systems can also be called
agreements or, in some cases, habits. Systems can be
large, such as company policies, or small, such as how

the receptionist is instructed to answer the phone. Systems can be formal (written instructions), but most are informal as people experiment to see what seems to work best. It is rare when what seems best really is best. This is especially true for management systems.

Systems and structure in the workplace can be considered living beings. They are the tangible and intangible structures that should help people feel supported as they work or go through change. Unfortunately, though, most systems are designed to give management the illusion of control over its workers, processes, and functions.

Although the data is clear, it seems to surprise most people to learn that *approximately 90 percent of the results produced in the workplace are a function of the systems, not the people who work in those systems.* Dysfunctional (fear-based) systems will destroy the human spirit in a workplace. What this means is that we can work on implementing powerful concepts like the Four Agreements in the workplace forever, but until we transform the elements of fear and control that live in an organization's systems into elements of love and support, the culture of the company will struggle to change while the results remain basically static.

Personal transformation is a wonderful thing, but transforming the workplace requires more: You must consider the systems in the workplace as well. To create the successful and supportive environments we've been discussing, you must not only look at transforming the people within those environments, but you must also look at enhancing their personal freedom, releasing the human spirit in the workplace, and transforming fear-based systems into love-based ones. If you want to change the results created in your workplace, you have to shift your systems.

## TWO REAL-WORLD SYSTEMS

I ONCE MET WITH THE CEO OF A $250 MILLION, fast-growing company that was having difficulty with its engineering department. New product designs were way behind schedule and didn't meet the customers' requirements. In a fast-paced, competitive market, this was a recipe for a major-league learning experience.

Upon reviewing the engineering department, I uncovered a number of systems problems and two potential management issues. The problems seemed fairly straightforward and could be remedied in about ninety days. I was scheduled to meet with the CEO and COO for lunch to discuss my findings.

At the appointed time, we met at their company cafeteria. When I went to get some soup and a salad, I had to reach under a splash guard and use a ladle in an awkward and uncomfortable position. Not being the most agile person in the world, I spilled some soup, which ran down between the pots and pretty much all over the place. After three or four tries, I finally got the soup into the bowl and the bowl onto a tray.

Meanwhile, an astute employee who probably does this all the time ran up with a special little sponge that fit between the pots. With incredible efficiency and a cheerful smile, she sponged away the mess I'd made.

After watching her for a moment or two, I noticed that my soup had dripped down the bowl, onto my tray, and all over my napkins. I went back to the napkin counter, got rid of the sopping napkins, and grabbed a few new ones to wipe up the mess.

Finally armed with a relatively neat lunch tray, my next stop was the cashier's station. After waiting in line for about five minutes, I paid my tab with a $5 bill and waited for my change. As the cashier began removing a few dollars from the appropriate compartment, the lever that held the bills in place came out along with the money. He reached in and pressed the lever back into place, but when that didn't work, he got a little panicky and pulled all the bills out. In his flustered state, he dropped one of the bills onto the floor, so he got up from his stool, bent down, and picked up the bill. He didn't want to give me the bill that had been on the floor, so he stuffed it back under the broken lever, took out another dollar, and finally gave me my change.

At long last, I made my way to the table and began discussing the engineering department with the CEO. He said, "What they really need is a kick in the butt. There's no accountability."

I said, "You're probably right on the accountability issue, but maybe we should look at your engineering *systems*. From what I've seen, it looks like they haven't kept up with your rapid growth and compressed time for new product introductions. Let's start by looking at the critical 20 percent of the systems that control 80 percent of the output."

He asked, "What do you mean by systems?"

I said, "Well, let's look at the systems in your cafeteria as an example. It took me three or four tries to get my soup into my bowl, and some of it ran into and between the other pots. That wasted a lot of soup and probably contaminated some of the other pots as well. Probably every time someone gets soup, the same thing happens, but you have a very good employee who runs right over and whisks away the excess. She was great. But then I put the soup onto my tray and some of it dripped onto the napkins. I got some new napkins and wiped off the tray and the bowl, but that certainly was a waste of napkins. I'm guessing that a systems problem is creating the spilled soup and other waste. The problem is probably that the splash guard is too low, the soup pots are too deep, the ladles are too long, or some combination of the three."

Then I said, "How long do you think we stood in line to pay for our lunch?"

He said, "I don't know, a couple minutes."

I said, "No, four and a half minutes. I notice stuff like that. What do you think it cost you to stand in that line? I don't really want you to figure it out, but as valuable as your time is, it's peanuts compared to what it costs your other two or three hundred employees to stand in that line for four and a half to five minutes to pay their bill. Why do you think we waited so long?"

He thought for a moment and replied, "We need to open another cash register stand."

I said, "Well, maybe not." I told him about the faulty lever in the cash register and how possibly replacing it might do wonders for efficiency. I noted that it's often difficult to see the source of our problems when we don't think in terms of systems. It would be easy to blame the cashier. But that's what I mean by systems. "Now," I said, "let's talk about your engineering department."

Until that day, this very bright and, at the time, incredibly successful CEO was completely unaware of systems thinking. Systems were invisible to this otherwise brilliant leader. Sad to say, this is still the case for many of our leaders in even very prominent organizations.

❧

ON ANOTHER OCCASION, I WORKED WITH A SOFTWARE company that was an absolute disaster. The worst division of all was the production area that warehoused and shipped the company's products. It was located in an old rundown building covered with graffiti, laced with broken windows, and surrounded by beat-up cars, some with flat tires. Trash was strewn inside the building and all around the yard. It was not what you'd call a great working environment.

One of the first things I asked about was the trash. An employee told me, "Well, we would put it somewhere except we've been asking for trash cans for two years and we can't get them." I asked someone to go through the building and find out who needed trash cans and what size they wanted. At lunchtime I went out and bought an assortment of trash cans. I spent roughly $69, but that small investment made an enormous shift in the energy level of the people who worked in the production area. People excitedly began picking up the trash and putting it into the cans they'd been dreaming of for two long years.

It took us about three months to redesign and renovate the warehouse systems, but that was just a "holding action" that stabilized the systems and allowed the division to perform at acceptable levels. Over the next six months, employees came in on weekends to paint the walls and spruce up the place. Morale soared. Employees also learned how to calculate the return on investment for other things they needed, like new phones and computers, and how to make a presentation to management to request the resources they required.

These people had always been valuable employees, but their spirit and performance had been repressed by unenlightened leadership and poor fear-based systems. Although re-energized, the people did not change significantly; only the systems did. And who changed the systems? The workers. They're the ones who used the systems, and they're the ones who knew what was broken or dysfunctional and needed to be shifted. As leaders, all we had to do was love, grow, and serve these people. In six short months, this department went from worst to first in the company.

Notice that the people could do little to improve the results they produced until the fear-based systems that prevented them from getting the things they needed were transformed into more supportive systems. Can you begin to feel the critical nature of systems literacy in organizational transformation, *especially in our new leaders?*

## TRANSFORMING DYSFUNCTIONAL SYSTEMS

DYSFUNCTIONAL SYSTEMS ARE FAIRLY EASY TO IDENTIFY, once you know what to look for. Here are a few of the most common ones:

*Merit Reviews.* This is a classic example of a fear-based system that almost everyone dislikes, including both the managers who give the reviews and the employees who receive them. Merit reviews are never "objective," as they're purported to be, and they create separation between managers and workers, and among workers.

*E-mail.* An incredible amount of miscommunication results from unconscious use of e-mail. This could easily be turned around with a systems change that required users to learn to write e-mail that comes from love. All words have energy and we should choose them wisely. We should become impeccable with our words, both spoken and written.

*Management by Objectives.* There's nothing objective about this management system. It causes people to focus on results rather than on the systems that create those results. Managing by objectives is like driving while looking in the rearview mirror. In a changing environment, this is no way to manage effectively.

*Meetings.* Poor systems have created inefficient meetings, which have proved to be one of the biggest wastes of time and energy in many organizations.

*Offices and Cubicles.* These structures simply create more needless separation.

*Top-Down Management Structures.* Designed from military models in an effort to maintain control, these relics of the past are long past their prime. Again, they only serve to produce more fear and separation in the workplace.

Prior to transforming your fear-based systems, you must first become *systems literate.* This means making the systems visible by providing basic training for all employees—especially leaders and managers—on systems thinking, and providing them with the fundamental tools for a systematic approach to creating a workplace that releases the creative human spirit.

Transforming dysfunctional systems can be achieved by following three key steps:

**1. Examine and Understand the Current Condition.** In systems work, the first thing you must do if you want to be successful is examine and understand the current situation.

A good way to begin is to do an emotional content survey. This type of survey identifies where emotions are running high. High emotions usually indicate systems problems. Don't just assume that because

Elizabeth is frustrated and doing a bad job, Elizabeth is the problem. The true difficulty may lie in the structure or system Elizabeth is forced to utilize.

When in doubt, always assume that the problem is a systems problem. You'll be right 90 percent of the time. It's not unusual for people who have been the most frustrated with their work to become your biggest champions in transforming the organization. If they don't, their lack of enthusiasm may indicate the presence of a people problem.

**2. *Focus on the Critical 20 Percent*.** A key premise of systems theory states that about 20 percent of the variables control 80 percent of the output. There's never time to address 100 percent of the issues, and there's no time to waste on the trivial 80 percent, so be sure to identify and focus on the critical 20 percent of the issues if you want to transform your systems.

**3. *Make Immediate Changes*.** After you've identified the critical 20 percent of variables that control 80 percent of your output, use that information to make immediate changes that achieve meaningful results. While tackling something big may seem more effective, it is more powerful to find something that will allow you to be successful immediately.

Instead of focusing on fixing your worldwide computer systems, go buy $69 worth of trash cans and clean the place up. The worldwide computer systems will be examined, of course, but not right away. The first step is to create quick victories and trust in your people for the new approach. Look for ways to praise your people, tell them how great they are at what they're doing, and measure their results so they can see the tangible proof of their efforts. Spread the word. Find ways to create immediate success in the workplace, and your people will support you.

⌘

OUR SYSTEMS HAVE NEVER BEEN MORE IN NEED OF repair than they seem to be now. It's time. It's time for transformation of the workplace. It's time for transformation both in ourselves and in our systems.

The antidote to unconscious behavior and our overstressed systems lies in releasing the human spirit in the workplace. The release of the creative human spirit is circumscribed by two major factors: We must transform our minds from fear to love, and we must transform our systems from control to support.

Transforming the workplace seems to come in two groups of threes. Personal transformation requires the practice of the three Masteries (Awareness, Transformation, and Intent). Systems transformation also takes three simple steps: Examine and understand the current condition, focus on the critical 20 percent, and make immediate changes. When that happens, you'll produce results that will be considered miraculous—with fewer resources and less effort than you could have imagined.

## STRESSED SYSTEMS EVERYWHERE

IN ORGANIZATIONS, STRESS IN THE BUSINESS SYSTEMS usually takes the form of stress on the people who work in, or are affected by, those systems. Excessive overtime, making the same mistakes over and over, frustration, anger, disruptive office politics, and low morale are all symptoms of stressed systems. People operating inside such a system will generally feel agitated or stirred up. Trapped in such an environment, their frustration eventually evolves into hopelessness and results in the depression of their human spirit.

Under the pressures of our current changing economy and business environment, including fear-based leadership in many organizations, America's systems of work, government, and community are incredibly complex and becoming more so each day. Complexity requires more energy to keep fear-based systems intact. Many of these systems are currently in a high state of stress, possibly the highest in the history of our nation, and we are already experiencing partial breakdowns that only add more stress to the existing systems.

Consider, for example, our systems for health care, education, crime prevention, criminal and civil justice, and government. With increased complexity and under the growing burden of layers of old solutions, these systems are stressed to their limits. It won't require a significant increase in energy to force these systems into crisis. Crisis is not necessarily a bad thing, because in a crisis, emotional content will be high. Changes that were vigorously resisted because of people's fears will quickly begin to manifest. Change will become an accelerating trend.

If we are to be proactive in creating our future, it's essential that we understand and correctly anticipate trends. When we understand trends, we can create an effective workplace strategy. This provides a powerful tool integral to every successful organization. A basic mistake many leaders make is assuming that the current economic or industry factors will remain unchanged or will change at a predictable rate.

Most people in America probably are somewhat skeptical that massive change is possible. Their old paradigm says that nothing can be done to change the "powers that be." In fact, the opposite is true: When the stresses become too great, *nothing* will stop the transformation.

An excellent example of this type of reordering is the change in the former Soviet Union. The old systems were as resistant to change as any in the world. People were sent to prison for even suggesting that things should change. Yet, when the last little bit of energy pushed the stress level to the reordering point, nothing could stop the process—not the army, not the Soviet government, not the bureaucracy, not other governments, not the KGB, not anything. All these heretofore impregnable forces became *irrelevant* in the new order. To be sure, old pockets of resistance remain, but their role and influence have changed forever.

For Americans, especially leaders of American organizations, this lesson should not be lost. We, too, have many pockets of resistance—old-time vested interests bent on keeping things unchanged and under control. We are rapidly reaching stress levels that will force our old systems to begin to reorder themselves. At this point, change, and ultimately, transformation, will occur at an incredible rate, and the old order will be totally unable to stem the tide of change. For those who desire to be proactive in this natural process of change, this is an exciting time indeed. I honestly believe this is the most exciting and meaningful time in the history of humanity to be alive and doing this work.

To take advantage of this wonderful opportunity, it's not enough to have the strategy and tools available for organizational and personal transformation; we must use those tools on a regular basis. We must incorporate the fifth New Agreement in the Workplace and learn to Practice a Little Every Day.

# 6

## FIFTH NEW AGREEMENT

# Practice a Little Every Day

*"The indefatigable pursuit of an unattainable perfection—even though nothing more than the pounding of an old piano—is what alone gives a meaning to our life on this unavailing star."*
—LOGAN PEARSALL SMITH

DID YOU KNOW THAT THE SPACE SHUTTLE IS OFF course approximately 97 percent of the time? It's true. The pilot, navigator, or automatic guidance system must constantly make corrections and adjustments.

The same thing is true in life. We human beings make a lot of mistakes, and we're frequently going in the wrong direction. We must chart a course toward our final destination and then navigate as we go, checking our position and making daily adjustments.

Every true path to enlightenment has specific practices associated with it. Different paths promote the use of different tools, and it's important to find the path that feels right to you. By finding your own personal path, you will be able to use the tools that work best for you. However, merely finding your path is not enough. The next step is to practice using those tools every day.

If the path you have chosen is the Toltec path, that means paying regular attention to the New Agreements and the three Masteries. If you've chosen a different path, make sure you know what its practices entail, and begin incorporating them into your life on a regular basis. Do you need to start meditating? Praying? Practicing yoga? Formal and informal practices, specific training, meetings, and support sessions are just some of the types of practices you may use with the path you have chosen. Don't be afraid to mix practices from different paths. *Do what works best for you.*

Like any new skill, mastering the New Agreements in your life and your workplace and making them something you do naturally requires regular practice. Without regular practice, your mind and the mind of your workplace will tend to fall back into fear before they can be transformed to love.

Practice your new skills and use your new tools in a sensible manner. Don't try to do too much. Strive for consistency. Incorporate these practices into your life in a way that gives you the best chance to stay on course every day. For example, if you're going to start meditating, start out slowly. Then gradually increase your time as you get better at the practice.

## THE ULTIMATE PRACTICE: WHEN IN DOUBT, LOVE SOME MORE

KEVIN MURRAY IS A GOOD FRIEND AND DEDICATED student of the Toltec. He's also a masterful teacher, a "go for it" person who puts his passion into his teaching and is willing to stretch in that role.

As the CEO of a successful company, he's taking this work into the workplace by forming small work groups with other CEOs. He has been teaching the Four Agreements and the New Agreements each month as a way to open the meetings and spur discussion on implementing the work in their respective organizations.

Kevin called me one day before his CEO meeting to ask what he should do if he found himself in a position where he wasn't sure how to respond as the group went deeper into the teachings. Grinning to myself, I replied, "Kevin, when in doubt, be authentic and love them some more. When we do this, we teach with Intent. With a little luck, we might spark an emotional energy field that comes from love, and the miraculous might stop by for a visit. This is really the core teaching of all true teachers. To teach these principles, we must live them. We teach what we need to learn. If we do this, we will be given all we need in our moments of 'unknowing.' A fully realized teacher is one who teaches through Intent."

The final piece of the five New Agreements is the fabric that connects all the agreements together. "When in doubt, love some more" means that when you're in doubt, you should love the fear some more. Embrace the fear, acknowledge it, and gently pull it to love. But do so out of a state of awareness and choice. We might also say, "When in doubt, practice the Masteries some more."

Remember that you can't love others more than you love yourself. You must take care of yourself first. In the world of business and the workplace, it is an act of self-love not to allow others to go against you. "When in doubt, love some more" starts with self-love and making choices from a place of awareness. It's not a call to set yourself up to be slammed by fear. If you're in a place where you can't express your love, and fear runs the show, start planning your escape. Remove yourself from unsolvable situations that go against you.

## LIVING WHAT WE TEACH

YOU CAN RECEIVE LOVE AND YOU CAN SEND IT. YOU can feel it inside, you can feel it outside, and you can instantly send it to anyone, anywhere in the universe. You can send your love in as many different ways as there are ways to express your humanity. You may express your love through thought, words, actions, prayer, practices, and of course, Intent. The act of being alive in the body is an act of love. Express it!

Send love to yourself, too. Be kind to yourself as you go through this process. We're always hardest on ourselves. Remember that you are always doing your best under the circumstances. Yes, you may feel that you're not always moving forward during this time of transformation, but don't give up and don't judge yourself harshly. Every step on the path is necessary and right, even when your mind may not agree.

## JACK'S COFFEE SHOP

NOW THAT WE'VE EXPLORED ALL FIVE OF THE NEW Agreements in the Workplace and looked at the fabric that connects them, let's look at an example of how they work together.

Not long ago, Carol went into a coffee shop with some friends. When the waitress finally appeared, Carol ordered a turkey burger with onions. When her burger arrived, *oops*, no onions. Carol turned to the waitress to explain the deficiency, but she had already disappeared. Carol waited. Then she waited some more. Finally, Carol waved the waitress down and pointed out the problem. The waitress became impatient and a little rude and started to hurry away. Before she could make her escape, Carol told her in no uncertain terms that she was a very poor waitress. Carol turned to her friends and said, "Do you believe this? That woman is completely rude and should be fired." Carol then vowed to herself that that rudeness had just eliminated the generous 20 percent tip she routinely left. She also decided not to return to the coffee shop again, as this was the third time she'd had problems with the service there.

Without awareness, Carol's mind did a number of things that created her unhappy reality. First, she didn't realize that her mind had run on free spool and given her no choices over how she felt or behaved. She practiced none of the three Masteries and violated all of the Four Agreements. She was less than impeccable with her word, she made assumptions, she took things personally, and she didn't do her best. In addition, she didn't see that this situation was, for the most part, caused by the systems in which the waitress worked, not by the waitress herself.

Here's what really happened.

Jack, the owner of the coffee shop, couldn't keep good help. He paid them minimum wage, with no benefits, and offered virtually no training. On that night, as usual, the coffee shop was short a waitress and everyone had to pick up extra tables. This made for poor service and overwhelmed the wait staff. In addition, the new cook was still making mistakes on the orders, and the wait staff was hearing complaints almost all the time. Management, in an ill-conceived effort to save money, only ordered food and supplies at the last minute. Poor inventory control caused the kitchen to run out of critical items, including onions, on a regular basis.

Carol's waitress, Doris, was the single mother of two children. Her ex-husband wasn't paying child support, so she was working two jobs, trying to make ends meet. She had started off doing her best to be a good waitress, but the lack of support on the floor, in the kitchen, and from management made her job difficult at first and now bordered on hopeless. On the night she waited on Carol, she was so stressed that she thought she might be getting sick. She was terrified about what would happen to her kids if something happened to her or she lost her job. She was living in her own little hell in the workplace.

Back to Carol. Without an awareness of what her mind was doing, Carol had little potential for choosing her thoughts or choosing to use the Four Agreements to shape her reality. Because she couldn't see that Doris's poor performance had a 90 percent chance of being a systems problem, she blamed Doris for the poor service and her unhappiness. Doris couldn't perform any better than the systems allowed her to. She didn't have control over the lack of help or the mistakes that others made. She couldn't control the rapid turnover of people or the lack of training. She was the victim of poor fear-based systems and domesticated management that was not only asleep at the wheel but also systems illiterate.

Let's look at another possible outcome. Suppose instead that Carol had become a master of Awareness, systems thinking, and Transformation.

Through her awareness, she would have quickly seen that Doris appeared harried and stressed.

With her expertise and awareness of systems, she'd note right away that the systems in which Doris worked appeared to be flawed in many ways. When her burger arrived without the onions, Carol would have wondered what systems problems might be at work here. Had she been unclear in her order? Was Doris unclear? Had the kitchen run out of onions?

Did the cook misinterpret onions versus no onions on the order? Was the cook new or untrained? Was everyone in such a hurry that they were stressing the systems and causing mistakes? Carol may not have known the answers, but she would have known that her lack of onions had a 90 percent chance of being a systems problem.

Now, to the Mastery of Transformation. Carol would have noticed that her mind wanted to blame Doris for the poor service. Instead, she could have chosen to look at those thoughts and see if they were making her happy. When she became aware that those fear-based thoughts were not serving her, she could have chosen to change them to something more loving. She could have chosen thoughts and beliefs concerning Doris that were more filled with love and compassion. She could have remembered that Doris was probably doing the best she could under the circumstances. She would have realized that it was highly doubtful that Doris was deliberately trying to give poor service. Carol could have reminded herself that this was a wonderful opportunity to practice the Mastery of Awareness and Transformation, the Four Agreements, and the mastery of systems thinking. She might have decided to see this whole no-onions situation as a blessing.

If Carol had followed these steps, she would have realized that she had the power to create a much more satisfying reality for herself. She could have remained centered and happy, even with the outside dream of fear swirling around her.

## FROM JACK'S COFFEE SHOP TO LOVE'S CAFE

LET'S TAKE THIS EXAMPLE ONE STEP FURTHER AND jump two years into the future. Jack, the owner of the coffee shop, has had a spiritual awakening and decided to transform his business into an enterprise with core values guided by love. After learning about and studying the New Agreements in the Workplace, he changed the name of his shop to Love's Café and decided to implement each of the New Agreements. Here's what happened.

**1. *Find Your Path*.** Jack and his employees decided that the path to love in their workplace would primarily be the Toltec path. In particular, they would practice the Masteries of Awareness and Transformation on a regular basis. Some members of the team were already practicing meditation, yoga, prayer, and other helpful practices, and everyone agreed to support those paths. This fell in line with the second New Agreement . . .

**2. *Love, Grow, and Serve Your People*.** As leaders, Jack and his team knew their role to love, grow, and serve their people. The team interviewed each employee to find out what support was needed. Importantly, the team also defined each and every one of their people as a potential leader. When in doubt, they would love their people some more. When in doubt, they would support the growth of their people professionally, emotionally, and spiritually.

Most important, this agreement went beyond work. Jack knew that problems at home were naturally carried into the workplace and vice versa. His support went into the home, too, when he and his team were invited in.

Jack hired people based first upon their commitment to their own growth and the growth of the team, second on the openness of their hearts, and finally, on their professional expertise and background. He hired warriors.

A big part of their growth led Jack and his team to the third New Agreement . . .

**3. *Mind Your Mind in the Moment.*** This third step was the centerpiece of Jack's transformational strategy, the Mastery of Awareness. Jack and his team knew that without Awareness, virtually nothing was possible in transforming their minds and thus their reality from a hellish workplace to more of a heaven on earth. In particular, they learned to use strong emotion as the trigger to remind them to become aware of what their minds were thinking, believing, and remembering. They became observers of their minds and made choices around what their minds were creating.

Of course, as they became better and better at minding their minds, their transformative process accelerated. This Mastery became the way they operated both at work and at home, and it allowed them to implement the fourth New Agreement . . .


**4. Shift Your Systems.** Jack had learned that 50 percent of the transformation he was seeking would be around personal transformation, and 50 percent would be around transforming the systems and structures that had so influenced his coffee shop. Through emotional content surveys, Jack and his team found out where to look for fear and control in the existing systems. They identified the critical 20 percent of the variables that controlled 80 percent of the outcomes. They moved from fear and control to love and support in transforming the systems, result ing in structures that supported their mission and intent. These first four New Agreements led natural-ly to the fifth New Agreement . . .

5. *Practice a Little Every Day.* Through regular practice, Jack and his team gradually evolved into that which they practiced. Their work became a model of the practices, a way of being. They personified the New Agreements in the Workplace. They became the Four Agreements and the Toltec Masteries. They learned to meditate throughout the day while living their lives, guided by their inner light and knowledge. They became their practices, and in the process, they became what they'd always been: love. It is this mag-netic energy that attracts others to their light.

None of these transformations happened over-night. In fact, the transformation from Jack's Coffee Shop to Love's Café required dedicated commitment to a deliberate three-phase project.

*Phase I: Stabilization*. The transformation from Jack's to Love's started with an emotional content survey. This tool let Jack and his team know how people, including employees, customers, and suppliers, *felt* about the coffee shop. Out of it they learned about the fear, frustration, and disillusionment of their people, customers, and suppliers. They realized that strong emotions probably indicated systems problems. They also knew that just the act of listening to how people were feeling would begin the healing process and build bridges toward enhanced relationships.

To kick-start the transformation process, Jack took all of his people through a transformational experience that "lit them up." This peak experience built strong emotional bonds throughout the organization. They became a family.

Jack realized that he and his team of people needed ongoing support and guidance if they were to continue to learn, grow, and be their best. He began working with Joanne, a New Agreements coach. In addition, Jack wisely made this type of coaching available to his people to raise their awareness, to make new choices, and to practice new behaviors during the Cafe's various stages of transformation. Jack laughingly referred to this type of coaching as the Cafe's "great accelerator."

Next, they identified the critical 20 percent of the issues that contributed to 80 percent of the fear in the business, starting with each employee. What was the critical 20 percent of the issues in their lives that created 80 percent of their fears? As Jack and his team worked to rectify survival issues around money, food, housing, and health and child care, attitudes began to change immediately. Fear was transformed to love and a feeling of support.

The next step involved looking at the systems that were causing the problems around poor service and customer dissatisfaction. These systems were readily identified and the root cause of the problems removed. At the same time, the team created new systems that were based upon love and support rather than the previous style of fear and control. Almost immediately, customer service improved dramatically.

Jack and his team had completed the first phase of the transformation from Jack's to Love's, a holding action that would stabilize Love's and allow them to begin the real work. Now they could depend on giving good customer service while stabilizing turnover and cash-flow issues.

*Phase II: Building Community*.  In this phase, the magic began to reveal itself. Jack and his team wanted to become more than a coffee shop. They wanted to become a valued leader in the community, a place where people could go to experience feelings of "family" and "home." This meant transforming their enterprise from a café to a community center, a place where people would experience love in everything they did.

To realize this phase, Jack and his team reached out to the community in whatever ways made their hearts sing. They built relationships based upon serving and supporting others in the community. Soon, people were coming to the café to spend time and support those who supported them. Love's served them food, drinks, and love. The whole environment was alive.

*Phase III: Releasing the Human Spirit.* The café is busy almost all the time. It now has a coffee and tea section where people can meet, talk, and browse the little bookstore. Jack will be opening more cafés this year in communities that have invited him to bring them the same value he brought to his own community. He and his team give frequent presentations in the area for small groups seeking direction in building their businesses or communities based upon love instead of fear.

By working on the three Masteries, Jack and his team found that they could implement the New Agreements and the Four Agreements as a model of organizational and personal conduct. With the mastery of systems thinking, they transformed their dysfunctional, fear-based systems to super-energetic systems based on support and love. The result was a coffee shop that created an energy field of love for both the workers and the customers. The food and service were prepared and served with love. Food prepared with love naturally tastes better, just like plants tended with love naturally grow faster. Equally important, people served in an energy field of love often experience both emotional and physical healing.

This experience of love caused the dining experience to become magnetic. Many more people came to eat and returned again and again to experience the love in the environment. The business earned more money by utilizing high-energy, low-cost love rather than low-energy, inefficient fear. Eating, serving, cooking, and managing became transformational experiences for everyone involved. Employee turnover virtually ceased, with people placing their names on a waiting list to work at Love's.

However, the most impressive aspect of Jack's success is the fact that he and his team have released the human spirit in their workplace. Their people are growing, transforming, and evolving at ever-increasing rates. Many have become teachers, mentors, or coaches at some level. They're walking their talk as models of what they teach. They are free to be fully human. They are working at the level of the Mastery of Intent, which means they are able to proactively create by aligning with love, the creative energy of the universe. They are whole, complete, and balanced, with nothing left out. They make no distinction between work life, home life, or any other kind of life. Every moment is life. And out of all this, they experience supreme happiness. Some have said that what they experience might be described as heaven on earth.

This is what can happen when you release the human spirit in the workplace. But it happens only when true and inspired leaders step up and point the way. In the next chapter, we'll look at the leadership skills that the changing workplace will require . . . and how *you* can become one of the new leaders.

# 7

# The New Leaders

*"You have come to this planet first to transform your own inner landscapes, to remember and love who you are. From that moment on, you bring light where darkness seems to be and bring love where fear seems to be. You are all in the business of transforming your planet. That is your real work."*

—EMMANUEL

WHY DO SOME ORGANIZATIONAL LEADERS FUNCTION brilliantly one day and appear incompetent the next? The most basic answer probably revolves around the fact that the world is changing faster every day. What worked yesterday may be the source of problems today. If today's leaders are not Masters of Transformation, then change will master them and their organizations. Leaders must not only understand and accept the need to continually grow and evolve, they must know *how* to do it. The "how" has become the transformative process.

A history of past organizational success often becomes a barrier to change. Doing more of the same things that used to work but no longer produce the desired results will cause organizational decline, especially as changes in the business environment accelerate.

For most people, it seems that the more we experience success, the more we tend to hold on to the things that brought us that success. A similar trait can be seen in businesses. It is usually difficult to change something that has been hugely successful in the past, even if it no longer works well. Just like human beings, business belief systems are often

based on past experiences. Organizational paradigms, especially past winners, tend to filter out new
ideas that don't "fit" into the current cultural con-
structs. Yet, if we live in the past, how can we lead
others into the future?

In the successful, love-based organizations I've
been describing, future leadership will no longer be
about control, manipulation, or domination. The enlightened leaders will have a deep desire to make a
contribution to all people, both inside and outside
the organization, and not just to stockholders or a
close circle of associates. The new leaders will understand that empowering, training, and growing
people is their job. By allowing and encouraging
the people in an organization to be the best they
can be, the new leaders also find themselves doing
their best.

Leaders of the future will provide guidance and
structure for their people. It is a leader's responsibil-
ity to develop a structure that guides people and
encourages them to be their best but, also allows

them the flexibility to improve and re-create the systems in which they work every day. Love, care, and
empathy, without supportive structure, can easily
cause an organization to become a dysfunctional
"family." A balance between the head and the heart
will create an empowered business "family" that is
energetic, productive, and most important, happy at
work. It is the coming balance of head and heart that
ultimately will allow the human spirit to fly.

Endowed with the spirit of the New Agreements
in the Workplace, the new leaders will be those who
take the knowledge gained from following their personal path and implement it into their professional
lives. To do so, they will need the courage to transform
their fears and commit to developing love-based companies. This requires a knowledge of the power of
synergy and the development of key leadership traits.

## THE POWER OF SYNERGY

MOST PEOPLE MIGHT SAY THAT WE ARE STILL IN
the Information Age, and to some extent, that's

certainly true. But information, however it is shared, is of little value unless it can be expressed by people in the form of creative energy. We are entering a new age, an age of conscious awakening, an age involving the transformation of the mind, an age of people, an age of planetary synergy.

In the book *Synergetics*, Buckminster Fuller talks about synergy, the principle that the performance of the whole is greater than the sum of its individual parts. We can think of synergy as emotional energy that comes from the mind. It is contagious and powerful.

Consider this. It is said in some teachings that in the creative process, thoughts, in the form of emotional energy, precede all else. Every thought flashes into the universe where it interacts with a "web" of other emotional energies, especially similar or like thoughts. As more like thoughts are created, more emotional energy is created. The increasing concentration of like thoughts creates an energetic "mass" of thoughts. As this thought mass accumulates, its energy begins to transform into a physical manifestation of that energy.

The greater the number of like thoughts, the more rapid the transformation from emotional energy (thought) to physical energy (creation).

Even more powerful than thoughts are words. The words we speak have powerful creative potential. Teams of people who think and say words with Intent progress even more quickly to the next higher level of creativity.

Finally, the most powerful creative power of all is action. Committed people in the workplace who think, speak, and act together *as one* create an environment in which miracles are created, the miracle of synergy. An inkling of this type of environment is the creativity that put a man on the moon. People working together, sharing knowledge, and creating synergy form the core of the ultimate cooperative advantage: *miracles*. Synergy is miraculous.

How would you like to have this type of energy among your co-workers, employees, teammates, or students? The new workplace will have that energy, and it will result in wildly creative and productive organizations. But transforming today's workplaces will require energy from many people.

## LOVE-BASED ENERGY FIELDS

AS EVOLVED LEADERS, WE HAVE AN OPPORTUNITY TO spark love-based energy fields in our organizations and our people. Love-based energy fields contain tremendous transformative power and synergy. Their power can dramatically speed the transformative process and should be incorporated in the process if at all possible.

If you were to ask me how to spark in a group an emotional energy field that comes from love, I would repeat for you my now-familiar refrain. I would tell you to love the people with all your heart, from the moment they come into your presence until the moment they leave. Oh, and one more thing . . . when in doubt, love some more.

Eckhart Tolle, in his wonderful book, *The Power of Now*, explains the potential role of the new leader in creating these energy fields of love. The word love can be substituted for his word: *presence.*

> *Group work can also be helpful for intensifying the light of your presence. A group of people coming together in a state of presence generates a collective energy field of great intensity. It not only raises the degree of presence of each member of the group but also helps to free the collective human consciousness from its current state of mind dominance. This will make the state of presence increasingly more accessible to individuals. However, unless at least one member of the group is already firmly established in it and thus can hold the energy frequency of that state, the egoic mind can easily reassert itself and sabotage the group's endeavors. Although group work is invaluable, it is not enough, and you must not come to depend on it. Nor must you come to depend on a teacher or a master, except during the transitional period, when you are learning the meaning and practice of presence.* (p. 87)

When the leader holds the energy of love or Intent for the group, others begin to feel their own essence, which is, of course, love. As more people feel their essence, the energy field increases. It's a little like making a batch of popcorn. At first nothing appears to be happening. Then the popping starts off very slowly. But as more energy is added to the environment, the popping becomes more and more rapid, with each popped kernel adding to the "fulfillment" of the container. Finally, with a rich energy field of love in full bloom, the real work of the group begins. Interestingly, it's the energy that does the transformational work, with no effort necessary on the part of the group members.

The beautiful thing about these energy fields is that they don't care about our differences. As a matter of fact, these fields begin breaking down our fears around our differences and human diversity. The energy fields don't care if we're white, black, brown, yellow, or purple. They don't care what language we speak or where we were born. They don't care about our religion or beliefs. They don't care if we're rich or poor, CEOs or new hires. The energy just does the work—a gentle pull that allows each individual to move at his or her own pace.

One of the universal principles of energy fields is that the more people who feel a particular type of emotional energy, the stronger the energy field will become. This is both good news and bad. The good news is that if the emotions come from love, that energy will energize them. Like attracts like. The bad news is that this principle also holds true for energy fields that come from fear. Fear-based cultures will drag people down—even loving people—into a spiritless sinkhole of despair. By practicing true leadership and loving with all our hearts, we can spark the love that exists in each of us.

## BALANCING THE FEMININE AND MASCULINE

HAVE YOU EVER WONDERED WHY WE SEEM TO HAVE SO much difficulty with relationships between the sexes? It turns out that this is a critical inquiry when looking at releasing the creative human spirit in the workplace. My work indicates that there are four parts of the human mind, and thus four parts of the organizational mind. I refer to these four parts of the organizational mind as the Masculine Mind, the Feminine Mind, the Authoritarian Mind, and the Spiritual Mind.

- The *Masculine Mind* is the masculine or male part of each of us. It controls our logical and sequential functions, such as speech, thinking, and reasoning.

- The *Feminine Mind* is the feminine or female aspect of each human. It creates our emotions and stores memories.

- The *Authoritarian Mind* is the authoritarian part of us. It sets boundaries and establishes rules, regulations, and policy.

- The *Spiritual Mind* is our connection to spirituality, nature, wisdom, and a higher purpose for work.

In general, women tend to be more in touch with the Feminine and Spiritual Minds, while men tend to identify more with the Male and Authoritarian Minds. However, for us to be whole and complete human beings, all four parts must be *balanced.* For the workplace to be whole, it too must balance.

## Achieving Balance
## in the Workplace

Two parts of the psyche tend to dominate the traditional organizational mind: the Masculine Mind (in the form of words, logic, and numbers) and the Authoritarian Mind (in the form of rules, regulations, and policies). These are the more male aspects of the psyche; they conform to the male organizational model that still dominates most organizations.

The feminine aspects of the psyche—emotional, intuitive, creative, and relational components—are typically in short supply in the business world. When organizations or companies struggle, it's usually because they're wrestling with issues such as creativity, teamwork, morale, customer service, loyalty, vision, mission, and a higher purpose for work. These aspects of ourselves do not exist in the Masculine or Authoritarian Minds.

The solution to these struggles lies in accessing the missing feminine components of the mind. To be Masters of Transformation, we must be masters of

THE NEW LEADERS

balance: We must bring into balance all four parts of ourselves and our organizational minds.

## THE HOLISTIC MIND IN THE WORKPLACE

IF ALL PARTS OF THE BUSINESS MIND ARE INTEGRATED and working in a holistic manner, the business is balanced, its culture is nurturing, and it is a place where individuals grow and prosper along with the business. The energy of a balanced organization is *complete*. However, most American workplaces are far from balanced. They tend to be dominated by the masculine and authoritarian, operating out of the old paradigm that values masculine influences, logic, data, authority figures, rules, regulations, and policies. The other two parts of the whole that are essential to its holistic power, the feminine and the spiritual, have traditionally been suppressed or even outright ostracized. The new leaders must begin to embrace all aspects of themselves if they are to create businesses that are balanced, whole, energetic, and wildly successful.

The process of creating balanced, empowered workplace cultures is twofold. First, as leaders we must become more balanced *ourselves* by engaging our feelings and discovering our higher purpose for work. Although men, in general, face the greater challenge, both male and female leaders must bring the feminine and spiritual aspects of themselves into balance with their masculine and authoritarian aspects. We have to become more comfortable with our emotions and feelings, and the *he* and *she* that live in each of us must move toward partnership and equality.

As the new leaders, we also have to become more in tune with the feminine aspects of our employees, and learn the importance of acknowledging and developing these aspects in an appropriate manner. This can happen only if we first balance ourselves internally. This is not easy! For many leaders, achieving an internal balance will be challenging. However, achieving this balance will become crucial to the success of any organization.

The second task involved in creating a balanced, empowered workplace culture is to create a higher purpose for work, a purpose that is in partnership with nature and universal principles. Those who are driven by a burning desire or higher purpose usually achieve great deeds. This purpose transcends money, security, or status. It is the knowledge that they are part of something worthy, right, and valuable. Only a small percentage of all companies ever realize their higher purpose. The ones that do, however, have a tremendous competitive advantage, since they have embraced the potential of the creative human spirit.

## ENTER THE POWERFUL FEMININE MIND

IN AN EMPOWERED, BALANCED WORKPLACE CULTURE, women are much more powerful and effective because they are able to be themselves. The traditional male-dominated, masculine-authoritarian business model would not exist if the men and women who controlled our businesses (and it's still mostly men) were balanced themselves. Sadly, most are not.

By suppressing the feminine and the spiritual in themselves, business leaders guarantee that they will suppress the feminine and spiritual in their businesses and the women in their workforce, including female managers and executives who don't suppress themselves to fit the male model. Women in the workplace who have overcompensated and suppressed their feminine and spiritual energies to fit the male business model will be challenged, too.

Organizations traditionally have required women to stress their masculine, logical, and authoritarian qualities at the expense of their emotional and spiritual aspects so as to conform to the traditional model. The business world needs women who are allowed by their company cultures to be themselves—whole, complete, and female. Otherwise, we all lose the intuitive, caring, creative, nurturing, emotional, relationship-sensitive side of ourselves.

A balanced woman resonates with personal power. She will use her ability to feel emotional energy to bring people together, to maintain harmony, and to create strong emotional bonds. Her contribution will emanate from who she is: the balanced, strong, and grounded female.

A balanced man will be a feeling man—strong, yet in constant communication with his feminine aspect. He will know about people and relate to them on a deeper level. This is critical for men, because in this age where the new wealth of the world is created by people working together, relationships are everything. A balanced man, like a balanced woman, will be guided by his higher purpose for work, and for life.

As we balance ourselves, our relationships with the opposite sex will improve dramatically. That's because we create the same relationships with the opposite sex as the ones we have between our Masculine and Feminine Minds. As on the inside, so on the outside. Transforming our relationships with the opposite sex both in and out of the workplace is not about *doing* something different, but *being* something different: a more balanced (and fearless) human being.

The process of transformation and balancing will naturally occur through living the New Agreements and practicing the Masteries. As the new mind becomes balanced and whole, it will create fear-resistant business cultures that empower and nurture relationships in all areas of life.

In working toward balancing the mind, it's important to remember that there is no winning and losing as there is in the current world of imbalances. Balancing is not about the feminine or spiritual becoming dominant over the male and authoritarian, nor is it about the masculine holding on to power. Quite the opposite. We need the Masculine and Authoritarian Minds *as much* as we need any other parts of ourselves if we are to experience being whole and complete in our organizations or personally.

Your mind may want to take sides in this balancing act. This taking of sides (fear) in the mind is exactly what's caused the separation and misunderstanding between men and women, both in and out of the workplace. If you find yourself taking sides, that would be a wonderful time to practice the Masteries of Awareness and Transformation.

As we balance, both men and women in the new workplace will feel safe, appreciated, and supported in each other's presence. They will be in touch constantly with their inner strength, warmth, and compassion. Women, ultimately, may be more often recognized as true inspirational leaders. A balanced workplace will have no glass ceiling for women. Sexual harassment will not exist. Men and women will be friends and partners without the risk of sexual compromise. In this environment, the feeling of family will prevail, and companies will benefit in direct proportion to the emotional well-being of their families.

## THE FEMININE AND CREATIVITY

IT'S NOT SURPRISING THAT MANY ORGANIZATIONS today struggle to remain creative in the face of a turbulent, fast-changing world. Often, we tend to search for creativity outside ourselves or, if we do look inside, we rely on the Masculine Mind to provide new thoughts. But new thoughts are not the womb of creativity. Creativity is birthed through *intuition*.

Intuition is expressed through subtle *feelings*. We have all experienced the sensation that something just "feels" right or wrong. The intuitive is usually attributed to the feminine, to women's intuition or knowingness, for a good reason. The feminine aspect of us, the Feminine Mind, is that part of us that *feels*. Intuition is literally, for both men and women, expressed through the Feminine Mind.

Three other synergistic energies appear to flow with intuition to gently nudge us into a creative state. Those energies are expressed as *openness*, *acceptance*, and *higher purpose*.

## Openness

Instead of trying to figure things out, open yourself to the possibility that you already know everything.

This is, of course, true. Because everything is connected, we are connected to all universal principles and higher knowledge. We need only quiet our thoughts to tune in to our universal knowing. Openness is a state of mind. Achieving it may require a little faith and practice in the beginning, but once you are open, new insights will flood in. However, they come with more of a feathery touch than the determined pounding of a hammer.

## Acceptance

Because of their subtlety, new ideas and feeling tones require you to be more aware and accepting of these messages. A big part of tapping in to the creative genius that lives in each of us means being open, feeling, and accepting while avoiding too much thinking or trying too hard. You may have noticed that many of your most creative insights come to you when you're worn out from thinking too much. Rather, *allow* creativity to happen naturally as you surrender joyfully to the feminine.

## Higher Purpose

The third important element that flows with intuition in the creative process is purpose, or more specifically, higher purpose. A pure higher purpose aligns us with the creative energy of the universe, which is Intent. Alignment *is* creative power.

If we examine intuition, openness, acceptance, and higher purpose as aspects of creativity, we can readily observe that it will be difficult to find these attributes in the masculine areas of logic or policy. A much more fruitful place to explore would be the feminine and spiritual. Intuition, openness, and acceptance reside in our feeling tones, in the Feminine Mind. Purpose and a higher purpose for work are found primarily in the Spiritual Mind. It is the feminine that brings new life to the world. It is also the feminine that brings new thoughts, new feelings, and ultimately, new creations into the organization.

## Characteristics of Inspiring Leaders

ANY TRUE TRANSFORMATION IN AN ORGANIZATION must have champions or leaders. Balancing ourselves and our organizations is an act of leadership, a new kind of leadership.

So, what makes the new leader? What values or beliefs are common among the truly great ones? People like Mahatma Gandhi, Nelson Mandela, Mother Teresa, and the Dalai Lama share a set of admirable traits and qualities including enthusiasm, patience, authenticity, integrity, generosity, and unconditional love. Similarly, poor leaders share a set of characteristics, too, but theirs are at the opposite end of the spectrum. These include traits such as being controlling, power hungry, abusive, self-centered, emotionally reactive, angry, blaming, arrogant, manipulative, deceitful, and greedy.

When you look a little more closely, you'll see that all of the positive traits stem from love, while all of the negative traits stem from fear. In other words, the great leaders are the ones who move us toward love and away from fear.

All we really need to do to move toward becoming a new leader in this world is to transform fear, and live our lives out of love. Again, this is where the Toltec Masteries of Awareness and Transformation come in: We must become aware of our thoughts, feelings, and behaviors, and choose to transform fear to love. Along the way, we will become systems literate, too. That's all there is to it.

Everything we are attempting to do simply requires the transformation from fear to love in our minds and our systems. All the great problems of the workplace, the environment, relationships—everything in the world—can be solved through this transformation.

Since you have chosen to read this book, you have already taken the first step toward being a new leader. As you continue on your path, consider the following questions:

- In what ways are you already doing a good job of applying the New Agreements in the Workplace?

- In what areas do you feel that you may have a little work to do?

- What actions are you willing to take to help you become more effective at integrating the New Agreements into your life and/or workplace?

- What support are you willing to ask for as you grow, evolve, and share your truths?

- If you weren't afraid, what actions would you take that would make your heart sing?

# 8

# A New Kind of Vision

*"Amazing grace! how sweet the sound,*
*That saved a wretch like me!*
*I once was lost, but now am found,*
*Was blind, but now I see."*
—JOHN NEWTON

IN WRITING *THE NEW AGREEMENTS IN THE WORKPLACE*,
I have attempted to make a contribution, to give back
a few of the many gifts that I have received over my
lifetime. I wrote this book in such a way that, hope-

fully, you would see me as a human being and a teacher, and become acquainted with me as a person. Anything that you experienced as real in reading *The New Agreements in the Workplace*, anything that moved you or made you feel at a deep level, lives in you. You and I are not different at our essence. We are the same, *one*. I am an aspect of you and you of me.

There's the story of the student who went to the Master and asked when he, too, would become a Master. The Master replied, "I am a Master. You are a Master. The only difference between you and me is that I know I am a Master and you don't."

We are all at different levels of mastery in our lives. We can say that at the level of the mind we are all in a process of unlearning our domestication so that we can own our personal mastery. We are Masters in the making. We are all Masters in the process of being enlightened to universal truth. Our job is to wake up to that fact, to *remember*, and to share our mastery with each other and with our world.

The greatest gift a teacher can bestow upon himself or herself is to release a student when the student has owned his or her own Mastery. We must, in the end, become our own teachers and teach our personal truth in a way that releases our spirit and allows our hearts to sing with amazing grace.

In meditation, I have seen that this is the right time to introduce this knowledge, that we will be supported in its distribution. I have also seen that *you* are the key, the vehicle that will speed transformation in the workplace and at home. Share yourself! Practice what you have learned. Follow your heart. Trust that you will be supported and that you are on the right track. Be who you are: a new leader in the workplace, at home, and in the world.

## No Turning Back

COMMITMENT *IS* TRANSFORMATION, IN BOTH OUR organizations and in ourselves. Commitment keeps us going when the going gets tough. And believe me, the going *will* be tough at times. Commitment is the drive, the belief so strong in a higher purpose, that nothing, no barrier or misfortune, can dissuade you from moving toward the bright beacon of a transformed life, an extraordinary life. Commitment allows you to embrace every obstacle as another gift, another learning experience, and another signpost on the perfect path. As Abraham Lincoln once said, "The probability that you may fall in the struggle ought not to deter you from the support of a cause you believe to be just."

Commitment is not logical or rational. Commitment is never victimized by circumstance. Commitment is who you are and what you stand for. Commitment is contagious and infectious. The commitment of the one can become the internal light for the many. So, whether you're climbing Mount Everest, building a business dream, fighting world hunger, or taking time to play with your children, your commitment to yourself and others will carry you through.

# Buckle Your Seatbelt!

Predicting the future has become a popular and lucrative endeavor. Many books that indicate the world is going to end have sold well. Tabloids are replete with predictions of doom, most recently even providing detailed maps that locate and describe specific disasters to come. Suggested potential sources of our demise include nuclear terrorism, global warming and other environmental disintegration, new drug-resistant diseases, violent earth changes, and economic and social mayhem. Every one of these things, and more, could happen at any moment. The good news is: *We can change all that!*

With the massive changing of our times described in this book, fear no longer will be allowed to rule the world. Fear is darkness and ignorance. Fear cannot exist in a space of illumination and universal truth. Franklin Roosevelt brought us partway in, telling the nation, "The only thing we have to fear is fear itself." Fear's greatest fear is that *it will be killed by love.* In its ignorance, fear cannot understand that it *will not die* but will be *transformed*—transformed into a love that is exquisitely beautiful and universally intelligent.

A global apocalypse is upon us. Not an apocalypse of the physical reality, but rather an apocalypse of the old, fear-ridden mind, specifically the mind of the individual, the mind of the workplace and the collective mind, the mind of the planet.

Mother Earth will have a role in this purging of fear. In the process of cleansing herself of the unconscious fear-based exploitation of her "body," she will assist humankind in facing our fears and evolving into a more compassionate and enlightened species.

The global future, created through our thoughts and emotions, pulls us toward a new reality, one based on the connectivity of love. The new leaders who will guide us through the process of becoming what we have always been will be courageous men and women who have already triumphed over their own fears and are now prepared to assist others who wish to make the journey. These leaders will appear in all walks of life, from a wide variety of occupations and circumstances. In the beginning, some will be recognized as leaders, but many will not. Recognition will not be an issue for these leaders; they will be doing their work from the heart, out of commitment and contribution to themselves and others.

Business, education, health care, government, and all people in all their wonderful diversity will begin to work together for the common good. No one will be excluded. Love welcomes each and every one of us with open arms.

Love will heal not only our minds, but our bodies, too. Understanding and utilizing the power and creation of emotional energy fields of love to heal the body will become commonplace. Most of us won't get sick, but if we do, there will be people to love us using both Western and Eastern healing practices. Education will be about teaching the truth to our children, our most precious customers, in a way that affirms and deepens their trust. Our teachers will teach through fields of love that will elevate learning to astonishing levels. Our children will become our teachers, too. Violence, drug and alcohol addiction, and dysfunctional families will become a note in history books as fear-based anomalies that have been gently guided into the light, transformed to love.

All this and much more is our destiny. As we transform the fear in our minds, the minds of our organizations, and ultimately the mind of our planet, our separations will begin to dissolve. We will experience our connectedness with one another, our living spaceship Earth, and our entire universe. National boundaries will begin to crumble. Our differences will be seen as good because we will know that we are really one, whole, and complete. Our humanness will transcend race, color of skin, gender, nationality, and beliefs.

Our experience of the future will be predicated on the emotional pull of love rather than the push of fear. Organizations based in love will pull supportive futures, which will produce companies that set new standards for prosperity while releasing the creative human spirit in the workplace. The emotional energy that we and our businesses radiate to the world will begin the process of creating a true world community of kindred spirits who have learned to work together in a whole new way.

The power of love is that it's never afraid. It knows no limits, and it will illuminate the darkness of ignorance wherever it shines. Love doesn't conquer; it gently embraces fear and guides it to lasting safety. Indeed, when you have experienced the power of love that lives within you, your fear that you will not succeed will also be transformed.

The time is now. We have this wonderful opportunity to support each other, learn these tools, work together, and love with every cell of our being. By doing so, by doing the work that makes our hearts sing in perfect harmony with each other and the stars, we can produce the miraculous transformations that will result in a new workplace and a new world in our lifetimes. We can. We will. It's time.

# WANT TO LEARN MORE?

For information on:

**Keynote Speaking**
**Organizational Coaching & Consulting**
**Coach's Certification/Training**
**New Agreements Workshops & Events**
**Emotional Content Surveys**
based on
*The New Agreements in the Workplace*

Call us at:
## 800-875-0506
Go online at: www.thenewagreements.com
Or e-mail David at: david@thenewagreements.com

∽∾

Want to Join Our New Agreements Community?

Want to Create a New Agreements Study Group?

Want to Send an E-Copy of the Book to a Friend for FREE?

And Much More!

Join us at:
www.thenewagreements.com

# SHARE THIS BOOK WITH OTHERS

## To order individual copies of this book (1–5):

**Order online** for fastest delivery:
www.thenewagreements.com

**Call** in your order at: 800-875-0506

Or use the Order Form below and
**Fax** to: 212-787-1676
Or
**Mail** your order to: The Emeritus Group (Publisher),
P.O. Box 237133, Ansonia Station, New York, NY 10023-7133

## For quantity orders (more than 5 books)
Please call The Emeritus Group at: 800-875-0506

---

**ORDER FORM FOR CONSUMERS ONLY (1–5 COPIES)**
Payable in US funds. Book price: $12.95 each copy. Postage & handling: US/Can $5.00 for one book, $1.00 for each add'l book not to exceed $8.00; Int'l handling: $9.00 for one book, $2.00 for each add'l. We accept Visa, MC, AMEX, checks, and money orders. Please, no Cash/COD. Call 800-875-0506, fax 212-787-1676 or mail your orders to:

| | |
|---|---|
| **The Emeritus Group** | Bill my: ❏ Visa ❏ MC ❏ AMEX |
| **P.O. Box 237133** | Credit card #_____ |
| **Ansonia Station** | Expiration date:_____ |
| **New York, NY 10023-7133** | Signature:_____ |
| Bill to:_____ | __Book(s) Total: $_____ |
| Address:_____ | |
| City:_____State___Zip____ | Sales Tax: $_____ |
| Daytime Phone:_____ | |
| Ship to: _____ | Postag/Handling: $_____ |
| Address:_____ | |
| City:_____State___Zip____ | Total Due: $_____ |

Please allow 1-2 weeks for US delivery. Can./Int'l orders please allow 2-8 weeks.
**This offer may change without notice.**